THE PRIVILEGE OF BEING CATHOLIC

FATHER OSCAR LUKEFAHR, C.M.

Liguori
ONE LIGUORI DRIVE
LIGUORI MO 63057-9999

Imprimi Potest:
James Shea, C.SS.R.
Provincial, St. Louis Province
The Redemptorists

Imprimatur:
+ Edward J. O'Donnell, D.D.
Archdiocesan Administrator, Archdiocese of St. Louis

ISBN 0-89243-563-1
Library of Congress Catalog Card Number: 93-79275

Copyright © 1993, Oscar Lukefahr, C.M.
Printed in the United States of America
00 01 7 6

To order, call 1-800-325-9521
http://www.liguori.org

Cover design by Pam Hummelsheim

Dedication

To all the friends
who have encouraged me in the priesthood
and have helped me appreciate
the privilege of being Catholic

Table of Contents

Introduction

Some time ago I attended a workshop in Southeast Missouri on "Being Catholic in the Bible Belt." During a discussion, the questions arose: "Just what is it that makes us Catholic?" "What are the distinguishing features of Catholicism?"

Different responses were given, such as our approach to the sacraments, our belief in the Real Presence of Jesus in the Eucharist, and our devotion to the saints. I became fascinated with the questions, and started to make a list of as many "distinguishing features" of Catholicism as I could.

The list grew into a series of talks presented to the priests of the Diocese of Springfield-Cape Girardeau. With their help, the list gradually found unity and coherence in the "sacramental principle," which states that created things are good and are signs of God's presence and grace. The sacramental principle is distinctively Catholic and is behind almost everything we believe and do as Catholics.

The sacramental principle is based on the Incarnation of Jesus Christ. Because God became a human being, we can be sure that human nature is good in God's eyes. Because Jesus walked the pathways of our world, blessing its people and all else in it, we can be sure that the world's inhabitants and all created things reflect the Incarnation and the goodness of God.

The Catholic Church in its beliefs, prayers, and practices has always proclaimed the Incarnation of Jesus. The Catholic Church has believed that God is present in the world, disclosing God's very Self in and through creation. From this, it follows that people, things, and events teach us about God and lead us to God. This sacramental principle has had a profound effect on the way we view God, the universe, ourselves, and life.

Reflecting on the implications of this principle has helped me to see our Catholic faith more clearly and to realize that it is a privilege to be Catholic.

To acknowledge that it is a privilege to be Catholic is simply to recognize God's gift in calling us to this Church. It should not make us look down on other churches. We should respect the sincere beliefs of others and see the genuine goodness in many holy people of every creed. But just as we cannot really love others unless we love ourselves, so we cannot really respect and cherish the goodness in other churches unless we first respect and cherish the goodness in our own.

It is my prayer that this book will help readers to know and to love the Catholic Church better and to appreciate "the privilege of being Catholic."

Father Oscar Lukefahr, C.M.

P.S. Thanks to all those who have helped me in the writing of this book... To Kass Dotterweich, who by her encouragement and enthusiasm helped bring this book to light. To Father Patrick Kaler and Cecelia Portlock for advice and editing. To Pam Hummelsheim for her expert cover design and interior formating. To those who read the entire manuscript and workbook: Paul and Carol Berens, Delores Lindhurst, Mellany Moyer, and Kathy and Dennis Vollink. To all who helped with various stages of the project: Father Anthony Falanga, C.M., Father Chuck Gallagher, S.J. (whose Parish Renewal Weekends helped me appreciate the privilege of being Catholic), Mary Almonte, Lewis Barbato, Jerry Buckley, Ben and Kay Burford, Paul Denson, Ron and Kay Gutru, David Hazard, Rick Janet, Henry and Jeanne Moreno, Joan Ruhl, Chris and Anne Smith, Pat and Sheila Thorpe, and Brock and Kathy Whittenberger. To the priests of the Diocese of Springfield-Cape Girardeau, whose insights and comments were so helpful. To the class at Saint Vincent de Paul Parish in Perryville, Missouri, whose enthusiasm and good humor kept me writing "on schedule," and to my sister, Joann Lukefahr, D.C., who made arrangements for the class and made many valuable suggestions. May God bless you all!

CHAPTER ONE
The Sacramental Principle

"When I saw my daughter receiving first Holy Communion," said Jim, "her white dress, the veil, her lovely smile...I knew God wanted me to become a Catholic." In less than a year, Jim made *his* first Communion, proudly walking down the aisle with his daughter and wife to take Jesus Christ into his hands and heart.

For Jim, it was a privilege to become a Catholic, and his experience spotlights something at the very center of Catholic belief. For us Catholics, the world is a sacrament, a sign that points to the presence of God and brings God's overwhelming love to us. Jim believed that God came to him in the smile of his daughter and in the body and blood of Christ. Catholics believe that God comes to us, speaks to us, and touches us through people and through all the good things of creation.

All the Good Things of Creation?

It might seem strange to talk about "all the good things of creation." Our world is far from perfect. Suffering, disease, poverty, famine, failure, crime, war, and death are a part of life. Faced with such evils, some human beings have written off the world and human existence as worthless. Some pagan religions have blamed evil on the caprice of gods, who "toy" with human beings for entertainment. Modern atheism denies the existence of

God entirely, seeing humanity as an accident with no meaning or purpose, viewing both good and evil as part of the ultimate absurdity of life.

In contrast, Judaism and Christianity see the world as having been created "very good" by God (Genesis 1:31). These religions place the blame for evil on us. The dramatic story of Adam and Eve, which is not just about the first man and woman but about us all (Genesis 2:4–3:24), teaches that human beings introduced evil and suffering into the world.

God has given us life in a world that could be a paradise. God made us free, intelligent beings and invited us to walk hand in hand with our Creator. God offered us the possibility of faithful commitment in marriage and the privilege of bringing new human life into the world. God asked us to use our freedom well, choosing what God declared to be good and avoiding what God declared to be evil.

But the first human beings "ate from the tree of knowledge of good and bad." Tempted by the devil (represented by a serpent, a common pagan symbol), they said to God: "You can't tell us what to do. We will decide what is good and what is evil." Through their choice, sin came into the world and developed a chasm between us and God. We became liable to suffering, to strife in human relationships, to fatigue and boredom in our work, to pain in such human functions as childbirth.

Unfortunately, we human beings have repeated the disobedience of Adam and Eve in a futile pattern of weakness and evil. What could have been paradise became a world hopelessly immersed in sin and death.

It was a situation we could not remedy. Finite human beings could not atone for the insult of sin against an infinite Being. We could not "reach up" to God and restore the relationship between ourselves and God any more than we could touch the edge of the universe. The love relationship between God and us could be restored only if God "reached down" to us.

God Touches Humanity
Through the Incarnation

The good news is that God loved us enough to reach down to us in ways we could see and understand. For eons of human existence, God offered love and forgiveness. One people, the Jews, led by Abraham, Moses, and other great men and women, put their faith in God, forming with God a covenant, an agreement to be God's people. They journeyed through centuries of human experience, at times lifted up by God's loving help, at times mired in human sinfulness. In all their ups and downs, they kept alive the vision of a restored humanity and a new creation, a "new covenant" of union between God and people (Jeremiah 31:31-34). Then...

"When the fullness of time had come, God sent his Son, born of a woman, born under the law, to ransom those under the law, so that we might receive adoption" (Galatians 4:4-5). The Son of God took on a human nature in the mystery of the Incarnation, God-becoming-one-of-us. "In the beginning was the Word, and the Word was with God...and the Word became flesh" (John 1:1,14).

From the moment Jesus Christ was conceived in the womb of Mary, a physical "point of contact" was established between God and the human race, a point of contact that could never be broken. When Jesus was born in Bethlehem, lowly shepherds could sense the glory of God. Elderly Jews, like Anna and Simeon, could see the hand of God stretched out to those who hoped for salvation. Magi could observe God's guidance in the light of a star that led them to the Light of the World.

When Jesus began his public life, human beings could look upon the face of God, hear God's voice, and feel God's embrace. In Jesus Christ, the love of God touched suffering humanity.

But evil still existed, and evil has always lashed out against the love of God. When God became human, evil found a "target," for Jesus had made himself vulnerable, liable to suffering and death. Enemies quickly gathered around him, and for many reasons, decided that Jesus had to be eliminated.

Jesus could have used his almighty power to crush his foes, but he had come to bring mercy to all, even his enemies. He refused to use force against them, relying only on love to call them to repentance. He accepted the terrible truth that if he continued to love his enemies, he would have to love them even to death on a cross.

And so it was Jesus Christ's love that saved us, an act of divine love made visible in a specific time and place when Jesus was racked with pain, tortured, and put to death on the cross. "No one has greater love than this, to lay down one's life for one's friends" (John 15:13).

But death could not destroy the Son of God. It could only transform the mortal body of Jesus into a spiritual, immortal body. Jesus Christ, as a human, passed through death so that his body was freed from the limits of space and time. On Easter Sunday, Christ appeared to his apostles so gloriously alive that even the most skeptical of them worshiped him with the words, "My Lord and my God!" (John 20:28) Christ formed his apostles and others who put their faith in him into a Church, a community of believers through which he would continue to be present to the world and touch all humanity.

Christ's death and resurrection underlined an essential part of his teaching, that we human beings have been created not only to spend our mortal lives on earth in union with God but to live forever as friends of God. Because Christ conquered the grave, death has become birth to eternal life, reforming our mortal bodies into "spiritual" bodies not limited by space and time (1 Corinthians 15).

If we put our faith in Christ and follow his teaching, he will bring us to heaven, which is actually the fullness of life for which we have been made. In heaven, we will enjoy the peace and love our hearts hunger for. In heaven, we will have friendship with God, with angelic beings God has created, and with all those people who have obeyed God's will on earth. This is our destiny as humans, and it is yet another reason why this world is a "sacrament." This temporal, material world points to an eternal, spiritual world where our restless hearts will find rest in God.

Christ Redeems Humanity

Christ's loving sacrifice of his life on the cross and his victory over death were the greatest events in human history. God's love created all in the beginning of time. In "the fullness of time," Christ's love redeemed all. We had been hopelessly separated from God, a condition symbolized in Christ's cry, "My God, my God, why have you forsaken me?" (Matthew 27:46) Now we can say with Christ, "Father, into your hands I commend my spirit" (Luke 23:46). Christ's love bridged the gap our sins had created between us and God. We are "redeemed."

Redemption, then, is the event of Christ's life, death, and resurrection which made possible a new relationship of love and union between us and God. We say "made possible" because God respects our freedom. God does not force love upon us. God only invites us to accept it. Until we do, we are snared in a condition known as "original sin." This condition deprives us of the union with God and the holiness granted to the first human beings before their sin. It weighs us down with the tendency to do evil rather than good.

God "wills everyone to be saved" (1 Timothy 2:4), and so we can presume that God offers all the possibility of deliverance from original sin. For us who are Catholic (and for many others too), the offer is made in the sacrament of Baptism, a sign given by Jesus by which the estrangement of original sin is replaced by our adoption as God's children.

Catholics believe that when we are baptized, we are changed in the very depths of our being. Baptism brings *forgiveness of sins,* deliverance from original sin and from any personal sins we may have committed. Saint Peter told the crowds in his first Pentecost sermon: "Repent and be baptized, every one of you, in the name of Jesus Christ for the forgiveness of your sins" (Acts of the Apostles 2:38, hereafter referred to as Acts). Baptism gives us the *life of Christ,* traditionally called sanctifying grace, and opens us up to God's assistance, actual grace. "We were indeed buried with him [Christ] through baptism into death, so that, just as Christ was raised from the dead by the glory of the Father, we too might live in newness of life" (Romans 6:4). Baptism offers *union with God,* with the Father, Son, and Holy Spirit. Jesus promised the Holy Spirit to be with us always (John 14:16), and promised also: "Whoever loves me will keep my word, and my Father will love him, and we will come to him and make our dwelling with him" (John 14:23). Baptism confers *membership in the Church,* the community of those who are united to Christ. "For in one Spirit we were all baptized into one body" (1 Corinthians 12:13). These effects of Baptism may be summed up as the new life given us by Christ, and this life will continue through our physical death as we are born to the eternal life of heaven.

"All of us, gazing with unveiled face on the glory of the Lord, are being transformed into the same image from glory to glory, as from the Lord who is the Spirit" (2 Corinthians 3:18). By Baptism, by God's grace, we become new creatures and are capable with God's assistance of performing genuinely good actions which are pleasing in God's sight because we have been remade in the image of God's Son. We become children of God, who are invited to spend all eternity with our God. (Second Vatican Council, *Dogmatic Constitution on the Church*, Section 7; *Decree on Ecumenism*, Section 22. Quotes from the Second Vatican Council will henceforth be cited as follows: SVC will indicate the Council; the title of a document will be given in full the first time it is quoted, then will be indicated by a key word, for example, *Church* or *Ecumenism*, followed by the section number.)

Catholics might ask, "Don't all Christians believe these things?" No. Some believe that human beings are totally corrupted by sin, and that Christ does not change us in the core of our being. Rather, he "covers over" our sinfulness and corruption. In this view, sometimes called "extrinsic justification," the sinner remains in sin, and even those baptized are incapable of doing anything meritorious in God's sight. There is no real change in sinners, but instead the merits of Christ are "imputed" to sinners without actually uniting them to God. In our Catholic view, on the other hand, God who made us "very good," remakes us in the image of Jesus Christ and joins us to the very life of God.

Christ Redeems Creation

We Catholics believe that Christ's life, death, and resurrection redeemed not only humanity, but in a very real sense, all of creation. According to Vatican II, Christ's redemptive work involves "the renewal of the whole temporal order." God "intends in Christ to appropriate the whole universe into a new creation, initially here on earth, fully on the last day" (SVC, *Decree on the Apostolate of the Laity*, 5).

Saint Paul referred to this renewal when he stated that "creation was made subject to futility...in hope that creation itself would be set free from slavery to corruption and share in the glorious freedom of the children of God" (Romans 8:20-21).

Catholics see the world, then, as "created and sustained by its Maker's love, fallen indeed into the bondage of sin, yet emancipated now by Christ. He was crucified and rose again to break the stranglehold of personified Evil, so that this world might be

fashioned anew according to God's design and reach its fulfillment" (SVC, *Pastoral Constitution on the Church in the Modern
World,* 2). Thus, the world, which was created very good by God
but damaged by human sinfulness, has been restored by Christ to
its original goodness, and then some!

Again, Catholics might ask, "Don't all Christians believe this?"
No. Even in New Testament times there were those who condemned material things. Paul's First Letter to Timothy speaks of
some who "forbid marriage and require abstinence from foods that
God created to be received with thanksgiving by those who believe
and know the truth" (1 Timothy 4:3). Today, those who feel that
redemption only "cloaks" human corruption are unlikely to believe that material things have been redeemed by Christ.

We Catholics need to reflect upon the meaning of Christ's
redemption of the created universe. There are many Catholics, no
doubt, who have never read the words of Vatican ɪɪ quoted above, and
who would be hard pressed to explain them. What do they mean?

Certainly, the air, the trees, and the sky are not "redeemed" in
the sense that human beings are redeemed. Inanimate things have
not sinned, nor can they possess wisdom and love. However, they
share in the "fall" of human beings and in our redemption insofar
as they are a part of our existence and awareness.

An example might be helpful. Imagine a prisoner, thrown into
a dungeon, chained to the floor of his cell. The air in his cell is
breathed into the lungs of a man in bonds. The oak tree visible
through the tiny window of the cell is beyond his reach. The small
portion of sky seen by the prisoner only reminds him of the
immensity of the horizons he cannot see. Then, a day comes when
the cell door is opened and the prisoner is unfettered. The air he
breathes is gloriously scented with freedom. He stands beneath the
shade of the oak and watches birds flitting in its branches. He gazes
toward the setting sun and knows that tomorrow he will see it
rising in the East. No longer a captive, he lives in a world which
is new because he is free.

In these ways, and more, Christ's redeeming love changed the
material world for us, who had been held captive in sin. Before
Christ opened the door of our prison, the air we breathed seemed
only to sustain us for a few short years, and then we were gone, like
grass which by evening wilts and fades (Psalm 90:6). The trees we
climbed as children, and formed into homes when we became

adults, were destined to shape the coffins for our burial. The broad sky sparkling with stars reminded us of the emptiness in our hearts that nothing on earth could seem to fill.

Then Christ died upon the wood of the cross, but rose on Easter Sunday to show that stone tombs and coffins made of wood could be gateways to eternal happiness. Christ breathed upon the apostles his Holy Spirit, and assured us that we were destined to live forever. The risen Christ ascended toward the sky (Acts 1:10) to show that our restless hearts will find rest and an immense joy foreshadowed by the vastness of the sky and the number of the stars.

In redeeming humanity, therefore, Christ redeemed all of creation. Christ made the world new again, because he transformed it from a prison into a home where we are children of God and heirs of heaven. He took all created things and made them building blocks for "a new heaven and a new earth" (Revelation 21:1).

Christ made, as we have seen, some created things into signs that would make him present to every age. Catholics call these signs "sacraments," and believe that through them Christ comes to us in ways we can see, hear, taste, and touch. Jesus made water a sign of the new life conferred in the sacrament of Baptism. He changed bread and wine into his own body and blood in the sacrament of the Eucharist. He inspired his followers to use oil in the Anointing of the Sick to bring comfort and healing. Catholics recognize seven sacraments as special gifts from Christ, and see in them another indication that Christ has redeemed all creation, for he has even made created things into "outward signs that give grace."

Incarnation, Redemption, and the Sacramental Principle

The Catholic understanding of Christ's Incarnation and his redemptive act has helped mold us as a community of believers. We may call this understanding the sacramental principle. It means that God is present in the world, disclosing God's very Self in and through creation. It means that people, things, and events teach us about God and lead us to God. It has had a profound effect on the way we view God, the universe, ourselves, and life.

Our faith in Jesus Christ, our view of the Church, and the way we discover God's will through the Bible and sacred Tradition are shaped by this principle. Because we believe that Jesus is truly divine and fully human, we believe that through Christ the divine and the human continue to meet through all of history. We believe that God invites ordinary human beings to form the Church, and we understand that the Church must be both a spiritual and a physical reality. We believe that God inspired human beings to write the books of the Bible, but that their human abilities and limitations are a part of the "finished product." We believe that God did not just present the Church with the Bible and then stop mingling with people; rather, God continues to guide the Church through human beings in what we call sacred Tradition.

The sacramental principle, of course, guides our approach to the seven sacraments, especially to Eucharist and Penance. We believe that Christ gave the Church these signs by which he would continue to be present to us, speak to us, and act among us. Because we believe in the goodness of things, we affirm that bread really can become Christ's body and that Christ really does forgive sins through the ministry of his priests.

Our prayer involves body and soul, and so our liturgies and traditional prayers include sacred signs and actions, as well as words. We use sacramental, sacred signs that resemble the sacraments, because we believe in the goodness of all the things God has created, and we believe that in many ways they can remind us of their Creator. We honor the saints, those who have died in the love of Christ, and pray to them because we trust in the goodness of people; we are confident that the saints will bring us closer to Jesus.

Our approach to theology flows from the sacramental principle. We know that human reason cannot fully understand God or the mysteries of God, but we believe that theology, our study of God, is capable of expressing spiritual realities in human language (whose words are signs) and of distinguishing truth from fiction.

Our ministry of Christian service depends on the sacramental principle. Because we believe in the goodness of both body and soul, we minister to the physical, as well as the spiritual, needs of people.

Our grasp of history reflects the sacramental principle. We look back at our history as a Church and trust that God has been present to the world through the Church, even though human beings in the Church have been far from perfect. We trust that God takes us as we are and can use us as instruments, flawed though we may be.

We find God in all the stages of life, and we have incorporated the sacramental principle into the way we approach old age, death, and life after death. This principle is an integral part of the Good News of Jesus Christ; therefore, it is essential to the content and manner in which we evangelize.

In the remainder of this book, we will see how the sacramental principle is at work in all these areas, and more. When others ask us why we Catholics do this or believe that, an answer can be found in our vision of the world as sacramental, created by God, redeemed by Christ, alive with the grace of God, a vision which can help us appreciate "the privilege of being Catholic." For God is found in the smile of a little girl. Jesus Christ is present in the Eucharist. God comes to us, speaks to us, and touches us through people and through all the good things of creation.

Questions for Discussion and Reflection

Had you ever considered the "Catholic way of seeing God and creation" in terms of the sacramental principle? Has reading this chapter caused you to see Catholicism in a new way? If so, how? In what sense is the sacramental principle a unifying principle, helping us to see why we believe what we do and why we worship as we do?

Can you think of some people through whom God has come to you? Can you name some things that have been signs to you of God's presence and love?

By nature, some of us are optimistic and some are pessimistic. The same can be said for philosophies of life and for religions. Do you think that Catholicism is basically optimistic or pessimistic? Why?

Have you ever thought of being Catholic as a "privilege"?

Activities

Make a list of mementos and keepsakes that are special to you. List some of the people, events, and feelings these items bring to mind. Then make a list of "Catholic things" that are special to you. List some of the people, events, and feelings these things bring to mind.

At the beginning of this chapter, *sacrament* is defined as a sign that points to the presence of God and brings God's love to us. The words *sacrament* and *sacramental* will be used throughout this book. You may wish to study the various meanings these words can have:

A sacrament in a general sense is a thing, person, or action which is a sign or symbol of a spiritual reality. In the Catholic Church, the word usually refers to one of the seven sacraments instituted by Christ, namely, Baptism, Confirmation, Eucharist, Penance, Matrimony, Holy Orders, and Anointing of the Sick; in these sacraments, Christ himself is present and acts among his people. (See Chapter Six.)

Sacramental, when used as an adjective, means "relating to a sacrament." *Sacramental* used as a noun designates a sacred sign (such as a blessing or object), which has been instituted by the Church and which symbolizes spiritual effects that come about primarily through the intercession of the Church. (See Chapter Ten.)

CHAPTER TWO
Jesus and the Sacramental Principle

M y first memories about Jesus are of Christmas cribs, stories told about his birth, and Midnight Mass. Every Advent, a corner of our living room would be transformed into Bethlehem, as my mother built rugged hills and a cave-stable out of boxes and colored kraft paper and peopled them with shepherds, magi, Mary, Joseph, and baby Jesus. I became one of the countless human beings who have been delighted by the story of Jesus' birth and by the carols of Christmas.

It is characteristic of Catholicism that faith in Jesus finds expression in symbols, story, and song. This is as it should be, because God, who is by nature beyond our ability to see and understand, became a human being so that we could look upon God's glory shining on the face of Christ (2 Corinthians 4:6). So we gaze upon the Child lying in a manger, we hear the story of his birth, and we sing of that "Silent Night" when Christ was born.

Trinity and Incarnation

Yet, doctrine is important too, as an explanation of what we believe. Our Catholic understanding of God's coming among us in Jesus Christ is expressed in the doctrine of the Incarnation, "God-becoming-flesh." This doctrine is itself rooted in Jesus' teaching about God.

Jesus spoke of God as Father, Son, and Holy Spirit, naming himself as the Son (John 14–17). In time, the Church came to express what Jesus had said as the mystery of the Trinity, three divine Persons in one divine nature.

The second Person of the Trinity, the Son, called the "Word" in John's Gospel, "became flesh and made his dwelling among us" (John 1:14). We know the "Word-made-flesh" as Jesus Christ, and we believe that Christ had both a divine nature and a human nature, united in one divine Person.

We cannot understand such a great mystery, but we Catholics believe that Jesus is truly God and truly human. We believe it on the testimony of Scripture and of the Church. We believe it because Jesus worked miracles, and because miracles still occur in his name. We believe it because Jesus rose from the dead, and in his victory over death we see the presence of God. With Thomas the Apostle, we acknowledge Christ's divinity with the words, "My Lord and my God!" even as we see his humanity in the nail marks of his hands and feet (John 20:24-29).

In New Testament times, some refused to believe that Christ could be God. Many of Christ's contemporaries denied that he was even anyone special (Luke 4:16-30), much less the Son of God (Matthew 27:40) or someone identified with God the Father (John 8:12-59). They could not imagine that God would actually become a human being.

Others denied that Jesus was truly human. Their denial seems to have been rooted in a rejection of the goodness of creation. (See 1 Timothy 4:1-4.) They reasoned that if material things were evil, God could not take on a material body. So they refused to "acknowledge Jesus Christ as coming in the flesh" (2 John 7). By the second century, some of these false teachings evolved into Gnosticism, which held that God was completely transcendent and unconcerned with the world. Material things and human beings were evil. Christ was a semidivine agent, neither human nor divine. Christianity rejected such heresies and subsequent ones which tried to deny the divinity or the humanity of Christ. Church councils, meetings of Christian bishops from around the world, expressed the official belief of the Church in the Nicene Creed, which Catholics still pray every Sunday at Mass. Jesus Christ is "true God" who "became man," that is, who became human, just as we are human.

We who are Catholic have steadfastly proclaimed both the divinity and the humanity of Jesus Christ. Acknowledging the Incarnation as the mystery of God-becoming-human has helped us to see the goodness of creation, and our instinctive grasp of the goodness of creation has made the Incarnation seem like just the sort of thing a loving God would do!

Divinity and Humanity Joined in Jesus

While we acknowledge both the divinity and the humanity of Jesus Christ, we come to know him through his humanity, because we are human. It was through Christ's human nature that his contemporaries made contact with Jesus, and it is still through his human nature that we encounter Jesus. His human nature gives us our truest insights into the nature of God.

The story of his entry into our world is related in the Infancy Narratives of the Gospels of Luke and Matthew. These gospels, using language that transcends history, tell us that God sent the angel Gabriel to Mary, a young woman of Nazareth in Galilee. Gabriel announced that Mary, engaged to a carpenter named Joseph, would have a child, the Son of God, by the power of the Holy Spirit. Mary consented, and Jesus Christ was conceived in her womb. His body began to be formed from the atoms that make up our universe. Nine months later, Jesus was born.

Jesus Christ's origins, therefore, are both divine and human. He had no human father, because he was uniquely the Son of God. Through Mary, his mother, Christ is "related" to the human race. The miraculous conception of Jesus in the womb of Mary was the moment when the immortal God took on a mortal body. From the moment of his conception, Jesus was both God and human, and so Mary can truly be called "Mother of God" (SVC, *Church*, 53). Mary, of course, was not the source of the divine nature of Jesus, but she was the Mother of Jesus, a divine person who possessed a human nature, and there was no time when the human Jesus was not God.

At Christ's conception, then, a mingling of divinity and humanity occurred that established the sacramental principle, for Christ became the sacrament of God, the sign that would make God known to humanity and make it possible for humanity to be touched by God.

Jesus Christ went through the stages of growth from infancy to adulthood. He experienced what we experience. He breathed the same air we breathe, ate the same food, drank the same wine, saw our sunsets, listened to birds sing, felt the caress of a mother's hand, sampled the perfume of roses.

Some scientists say that because of the dispersion of molecules in the atmosphere around us, every breath we take in contains a molecule once breathed by Jesus! The air we breathe and the universe we call home have been blessed by the presence of Christ.

Jesus and the Catholic Sacramental Principle

Study of Christ's life and of his approach to material things can bring us to a better understanding of the Catholic sacramental principle. Everything Jesus Christ did put God's stamp of approval on human life and the created world.

Jesus chose to be born into a family which possessed neither power, nor wealth, nor fame, as if to show that human existence needs none of these things to have value. He spent his first thirty years performing everyday tasks and living an ordinary family life, as if to indicate that these things are so good that God could find nothing more important to do!

The stories Jesus told show us that he loved nature and the ordinary things of life. He spoke of the sun and rain, wildflowers and trees, birds and foxes, people building houses and farmers planting crops, women baking bread and fishermen casting their nets (Matthew 5–7; 13). He worked miracles to provide wine for a party and food for those who listened to him (John 2:1-11; 6:1-13). There can be no doubt that Jesus saw the world and all created things as "very good."

Jesus and the Church

Jesus loved people, and he was lovable, for little children sought his embrace and people kept inviting him to meals. He searched out people like the blind Bartimaeus who were neglected by others (Mark 10:46-52). He paid attention to a poor widow nobody else noticed (Mark 12:41-44). Even despised sinners like

Zacchaeus the tax collector were important to Jesus (Luke 19:1-10).

Jesus trusted people to share his ministry. He called twelve apostles and seventy-two disciples to go before him preaching the Good News (Luke 9:1-6; 10:1-12). He spoke of building his Church on one of the Twelve (Matthew 16:18), and even after Peter denied him three times, he gave Peter a threefold commission to shepherd the flock of the Church (John 21:15-19).

Jesus saw people as good, even when they sometimes failed him. He is portrayed in the gospels as building a Church of sinful people prone to failure, yet dearly loved by Jesus as his friends (John 15:15). He said that his kingdom was not of this world in the sense that he was not interested in worldly power or dominance (John 18:36), but the gospels show that he wanted to form a Church which would be visible because it would be composed of real human beings.

Jesus, the Bible, and Tradition

Jesus knew Scripture (John 7:14), read the Old Testament as God's Word, and explained some passages as referring to himself (Luke 4:16-21; 24:27). Jesus said to his disciples, "Whoever listens to you listens to me" (Luke 10:16), indicating that God's Word is also addressed to the world through the teaching of the apostles.

Jesus thus led the Catholic Church to discover God's Word in the Bible and in sacred Tradition, our expression for the reality of God's continuing guidance of the Church. In both Bible and sacred Tradition, God sees people as suitable instruments to bring truth to the world.

Jesus and the Sacraments

Jesus began his public ministry with his baptism in the Jordan River by John, his cousin (Luke 3:21-22). The sinless Jesus did not need a baptism signifying forgiveness of sins, but this event showed that he approved of signs and symbols that point to spiritual realities.

He went much further than mere symbolism when he took bread and said, "This is my body" (Matthew 26:26), and when he said to his apostles, "Whose sins you forgive are forgiven them" (John 20:23). He created what we Catholics call sacraments, signs which actually convey God's grace.

Jesus, Prayer, Sacramentals, and Saints

Jesus prayed with his body, as well as with his heart and mind. He went on pilgrimage to Jerusalem with Mary and Joseph (Luke 2:42). He fasted in the desert for forty days (Luke 4:1-2). He looked up to heaven as he blessed food (Luke 9:16). He prayed in solitude (Luke 9:18) and in the hearing of his disciples (Luke 10:21-22). He taught his followers to ask for bodily needs like bread, as well as spiritual needs like forgiveness (Luke 11:2-4). He prayed in agony (Luke 22:39-46), and he prayed at the hour of his death (Luke 23:46).

Modeling our prayer on that of Jesus, we Catholics pray in many ways that involve the whole person. We come before God not as disembodied spirits, but as human beings with bodily and spiritual needs.

Our Catholic use of sacramentals, which are signs and blessings that remind us of God, may be traced back to Jesus' use of things and to his prayers of blessing. He used soil, saliva, and water to effect a healing (John 9). At the Jewish feast of Tabernacles, when four great torches were lit to illuminate the Temple Court of Women, Jesus called himself the Light of the World (John 7:1–8:12). He celebrated the Passover ritual, with its many beautiful signs and blessings (Luke 22:7-16). We, too, pray, using signs, symbols, and prayers of blessing.

Our Catholic tradition of praying to the saints finds its roots in the life of Jesus. The event of the transfiguration, when Jesus appeared in glory conversing with Moses and Elijah about his coming death in Jerusalem (Luke 9:28-36), indicates that there is interaction among those in heaven and us on earth. His mother's intervention at the wedding feast of Cana has encouraged Catholics to seek Mary's intercession in prayer (John 2:1-11). When Jesus entrusted his mother to the beloved disciple (John 19:26-27), he entrusted her, we believe, to all those who are beloved disciples. The willingness with which Jesus responded to the spoken and unspoken requests of those he loved on earth (John 11) leads us to believe that he responds to the requests of those he loves in heaven.

Jesus, Theology, Service, and History

Jesus taught by using parables, but he also explained his stories (Matthew 13). He showed the difference between truth and falsehood, and taught with authority (Matthew 7:24-29). He was not afraid to make difficult moral demands of his followers (Mark 10:1-12). In such ways, Christ inspired us to believe in the importance of correct doctrine, of stating truth as clearly as possible, and of being faithful to the truth no matter how difficult it may be. In short, Christ laid the groundwork for theology, the study of God and of God's truth.

Jesus came to bring us to eternal life in heaven; he ministered to others by forgiving sins (Mark 2:5) and promising paradise (Luke 23:43). But Jesus also cared about our mortal life here on earth. He healed the body, as well as the spirit (Mark 2:11). He fed the hungry and gave drink to the thirsty, even caring about things that might seem unessential. Indeed, the first miracle Jesus worked, according to John's Gospel, was supplying fine wine in huge quantities to keep a party going, and his last action as described in John's Gospel was fixing breakfast for his apostles (John 21:1-13). In imitation of Christ, the Catholic Church has tried to serve the spiritual and the physical needs of human beings.

Jesus entered into human history, and thereby showed that the story of human beings, flawed as it is, is cherished by God. Jesus belonged to a certain people, the Jews, who in their sacred writings indicated that God intervenes in human history. Jesus told his apostles that he would be with them always, demonstrating that he would be involved in their future. Since Christ was so willing to be a part of the history of sinful people, we Catholics do not consider it presumptuous to find him in ours.

Jesus and the Stages of Life

Jesus spent nine months in the womb of his mother. He went through the stages of infancy, childhood, and adolescence. He grew into adulthood. Because he gave his life for us on the cross, Jesus did not attain old age. But he endured anguish, dreadful pain, and a terrifying death. Christ experienced human life, from conception through death. He taught us that every moment of human life can be holy, and that we can share every moment of our lives with him. Finally, Christ's life, death, and resurrection is a sacrament, a sign, showing us that our mortal life is destined to be transformed into eternal life, proclaiming that our true purpose in life is loving union with God that will last forever.

Jesus and Evangelization

Perhaps nothing shows the confidence Jesus placed in his followers more than his approach to evangelization, the spread of the gospel. When Jesus ascended into heaven, only a few people, most of them Jews, had even heard of him. He entrusted the gospel to his followers: "Go, therefore, and make disciples of all nations, baptizing them in the name of the Father, and of the Son, and of the holy Spirit, teaching them to observe all that I have commanded you" (Matthew 28:19-20).

We who are Catholic believe that Jesus asks us to spread the gospel. We believe that we can best accomplish his purposes when we have his attitude toward material things and toward people.

Christmas: Incarnation and the Sacramental Principle

But back to Christmas cribs....Legend says that Saint Francis of Assisi made the first crib as a sign of his belief in the Incarnation. It seems appropriate that this great lover of Jesus Christ was also a lover of animals and all created things. Like Francis, one of our Catholic saints, we are invited as Catholics to believe wholeheartedly in Jesus Christ as God and human. We are privileged to find Christ in all those Catholic signs that reflect both his divinity and his humanity.

Questions for Discussion and Reflection

What are your first memories of Jesus Christ? What symbols, stories, and songs have been important to your religious and spiritual development?

Can you express the Catholic understanding of the Trinity, the Incarnation, and the Redemption in clear terms? Why is an understanding of these doctrines crucial to our understanding of Jesus himself?

The text listed some gospel passages which indicate Jesus' love of nature and of people. Can you think of any others?

Can you express in your own words how the life and teaching of Jesus helped form the sacramental principle of the Catholic Church and its application in these areas: Church, Bible and sacred Tradition, sacraments, prayer, sacramentals, saints, theology, service, history, stages of life, and evangelization?

Activities

Go to a quiet place where you can be alone. Relax and reflect on the presence of God for a few moments. Close your eyes and breathe deeply. Consider the fact that you are breathing molecules of air once breathed by Jesus Christ. Think of the things you enjoy most in nature and imagine Jesus sitting by your side, enjoying them with you. Ask Jesus to help you realize that he really is at your side, and within you, and that everything you do can be done in union with him.

CHAPTER THREE
The Church, Sacrament of Jesus

After joining the human race, being born at Bethlehem, dying on the cross, and rising from the dead, what could Jesus Christ have done for an encore?

He could, of course, have continued his physical presence on earth, appearing daily to those who believed in him, healing the sick, comforting the afflicted, teaching those eager to learn.

But he didn't. Instead, Jesus involved his followers in his mission of bringing God's love, forgiveness, and grace to the world. Jesus made his followers children of his heavenly Father, and poured the Holy Spirit into their hearts. With the Father and the Holy Spirit, Jesus began to dwell in those who were baptized in his name. This "indwelling" was so real that Jesus could identify himself with his followers. "Saul, Saul, why are you persecuting *me*?" he asked in a stunning revelation which turned a foe into an ardent disciple (Acts 9:1-30). That disciple, later known as Paul, would write to Christians: "You are Christ's body" (1 Corinthians 12:27). He would explain that Christ "is the head of the body, the church" (Colossians 1:18).

The Incarnation Continued

Christ was born into the world at Bethlehem to "incarnate" God's presence, to unite divinity to a human nature. Truly God,

Jesus Christ was also fully human. Before Jesus was crucified, he had a mortal body through which he could listen, speak, touch, forgive, heal, share, pray, love, unite, and bless. After his Resurrection and Ascension, he chose to continue doing these things through his followers. They were to be his hands and heart.

That is why Catholics believe that Christ's Church is more than an invisible communion of faith. Just as Christ had a real physical body, so Christ's Church is made up of a real physical union of believers held together by human bonds, as well as by divine grace. The Church is the "Mystical Body of Christ" (SVC, *Church*, 7–8), an expression which reflects both the spiritual ("Mystical") and the physical ("Body") nature of the Church.

Some Christians see the human, physical side of the Church as a barrier between them and God. They contend that the Church should be only a spiritual—and therefore invisible—community of faith. God offers grace, they think, directly to each person, not through the "mediation" of any Church. God speaks, they suppose, to each one individually, not through the teaching office of a Church.

But the Bible shows that God offers salvation to human beings "not merely as individuals without any mutual bonds, but by making them into a single people." First, God formed the people of Israel to prepare the way, then through Jesus Christ, he formed the new "people of God" (1 Peter 2:10). This "People of God" is the Church (SVC, *Church*, 9).

Two thousand years ago, some people saw the physical body of Jesus as a stumbling block. When Jesus, for example, forgave the sins of a paralyzed man, some objected: "Why does this man speak that way? He is blaspheming. Who but God alone can forgive sins?" (Mark 2:7) It is true that only God can forgive sins. What they could not comprehend was that Christ is God.

In a similar way, those who object to a visible Church do not realize what Catholics believe, that God is present in the Church and that Christ ministers to the world through the Church. This is a special insight of Catholicism, the awareness that the Incarnation continues as Christ comes to the world through his Body, the Church. The Church is not a "go-between" through which people contact Christ. The Church is a sacrament, a sign, in which Christ is truly present, just as God was truly present in Christ during his mortal life on earth. "Whoever listens to you," said Jesus, "listens to me. Whoever rejects you rejects me. And whoever rejects me rejects the one who sent me" (Luke 10:16).

The Origins of the Church

The Church as a spiritual and physical community finds its origin in Jesus himself. The first generation of Christians believed that Christ intended to establish a Church. "You are Peter," Jesus said to the first among his apostles, "and upon this rock I will build my church" (Matthew 16:18). He intended his Church to have leaders who would make decisions ratified by God: "Whatever you bind on earth shall be bound in heaven, and whatever you loose on earth shall be loosed in heaven" (Matthew 18:18). They believed that Christ gave them ritual observances by which to remember him: "This is my body, which will be given for you; do this in memory of me" (Luke 22:19). They accepted from Jesus strict rules of conduct (Matthew 5:21-22) and guidelines for marriage (Mark 10:2-12). They believed that Jesus expected his followers to have standards for membership in the Church, and that those who violated them were to be excluded (Matthew 18:17). All these Scripture passages point to a Church which is physical and visible.

Catholics accept the reality of such a Church because it is in keeping with the Incarnation itself. Just as God became visible through Jesus Christ, so Christ is visible today through his Church. Even though the human beings which make up the Church are imperfect, they are, the Catholic Church believes, redeemed by Christ and renewed in the image of Christ. Besides, Christ was known for loving sinners and enabling them by grace to accomplish great things!

Jesus was aware that the ones he chose to represent him were subject to failure. The apostles ran away when Jesus was arrested, and Peter denied Jesus three times. In the early Church, there were liars and hypocrites (Acts 5:1-11). There were complaints of unfairness (Acts 6:1). There were those who used religion for personal gain (Acts 8:9-24). There were disagreements about doctrine (Acts 15). There were conflicts among Church leaders (Acts 15:36-41). There were sermons that failed to impress the preacher's audience (Acts 17:22-34) and sermons that put people to sleep (Acts 20:7-12). There were questions about pastors' salaries, disorder at worship ceremonies, lust and scandal, and neglect of the poor (1 Corinthians 5-11).

Christ, then, did not found a Church of angels, of perfect spiritual beings. He established a Church of flesh-and-blood people who could and did fail. Yet, these people were the very ones addressed in the Bible as the Body of Christ. Christ used imperfect human beings to continue his presence two thousand years ago. He continues his presence today through members of his Church who are in need of "continual reformation" (SVC, *Ecumenism*, 6).

Membership in the Church

The Second Vatican Council states our belief that the "one true religion subsists in the catholic and apostolic Church" (SVC, *Declaration on Religious Freedom*, 1). "They are fully incorporated into the society of the Church who, possessing the Spirit of Christ, accept her entire system and all the means of salvation given to her, and through union with her visible structure are joined to Christ, who rules her through the Supreme Pontiff and the bishops" (SVC, *Church*, 14).

But the Church recognizes that we are "linked with those who, being baptized, are honored with the name of Christian," even if they are not fully incorporated into the Church (SVC, *Church*, 15). We are related also to people who believe in God or seek for God. God does not deny the help necessary for salvation to those who, through no fault of their own, do not have an explicit knowledge of God. They can find salvation if they strive, with the help of God's grace, to lead a good life; their salvation comes from Christ, even though they do not know him (SVC, *Church*, 16).

Catholics, therefore, recognize a certain unity with all people of good will, and see much goodness in other churches. At the same time, we believe that it is only in the Catholic Church that "the fullness of the means of salvation can be obtained" (SVC, *Ecumenism*, 3). This is based on our realization that salvation comes from Christ alone, and that only the Catholic Church has all those means given by Christ to teach, govern, and sanctify humanity.

One, Holy, Catholic, Apostolic Church

The Catholic Church has those means because it is *one* with the Church Christ founded. It is built on the rock of Peter's faith (Matthew 16,18) and is one under Peter's successor, the pope. The unity we have had throughout the world and through the centuries is our assurance that Christ gives grace through the Church today.

The Church is *holy*. "You are...'a holy nation'" (1 Peter 2:9). This does not mean that we are sinless, but that Christ gives us a share in his holiness through Baptism, and forgives our sins when we repent of them. Christ does not, as some think, merely "cover over" our sinfulness. He is "the Lamb of God, who takes away the sin of the world" (John 1:29). He offers us, through the Church, the means to lead a holy life in union with him (Philippians 1:4-11).

The Church is *catholic*. This word, first used in reference to Christians by Saint Ignatius of Antioch around A.D. 100, means "universal" and indicates that Christ's Church is meant for the whole world. When divisions arose among followers of Christ, "Catholic" became a name; thus, Saint Augustine spoke of himself as a Catholic Christian. In our union with Catholic believers throughout the world, we see a safeguard against error and division.

The Church is *apostolic*. This means that the Church traces its authority back to Jesus through the apostles. Jesus commissioned the apostles (Acts 1:8; 9:15), who commissioned others (2 Timothy 1:6) who did the same through the centuries up to the pope and bishops today. The Church is apostolic also because it faithfully proclaims the teaching of the apostles and ministers the sacraments given by Christ to the apostles.

The unity, holiness, catholicity, and apostolicity of the Catholic Church are related to the sacramental principle, to our belief in the goodness of creation and people. As human beings, we see the need for a visible sign of unity, the pope, and we trace that unity back through Peter to Christ. We believe that God can share holiness with people without detracting from the divine holiness. (Some Christians believe that we cannot credit holiness to human beings without diminishing the holiness of God.) We find in our call to be catholic a mandate from God to serve all people as God's beloved children. We are convinced that Christ founded the Church on the apostles (Ephesians 2:20), not just for one generation but for all. The visible succession of bishops is a constant reminder that grace comes from Christ, not from us, for through this succession we trace all ministry in the Church back to Christ himself.

"Safety in Numbers"

We Catholics believe in a visible Church because we are convinced that it was intended by Jesus Christ. We also see the wisdom, in any endeavor involving human beings, of belonging to a group. Some Christians follow the principle that the individual stands alone before God and that each believer is entitled to interpret the Bible without any reference to a Church. This sounds very democratic, but as history has shown, it leads to a proliferation of churches and to a splintering of the unity for which Christ prayed (John 17:21).

We have all heard the expression, "common sense." It means that down-to-earth reality and truth can be found where the community agrees. The Catholic Church believes that the community as such is led by the Holy Spirit, and that individual members are far more likely to arrive at truth when they seek it in community. We believe that individuals receive the Holy Spirit at Baptism, but we realize that individuals can easily deceive themselves into thinking that God is speaking when they are actually listening to their own pride or foolishness. Individual "inspirations," then, must always be verified through the wisdom of the community, through the teaching given by the Church.

The whole Catholic community shares in the priesthood of Christ, in the offices of teaching, governing, and sanctifying (SVC, *Church*, 10). Catholics exercise these responsibilities subject to the "common sense" of the community under the guidance of the Holy Spirit.

Ordained ministers in the Catholic Church—bishops, priests, and deacons—participate in the priesthood of Christ in a unique way, and derive their authority from Christ. But they come from the whole community of the Church and have a responsibility toward the whole Church. Thus, the entire community is blessed by the gifts given to each individual. This does not guarantee that leaders and other members of the Church will not make mistakes, but it does offer the best possible human assurance that the Church will be faithful and prudent in bringing Christ to the world.

Christ Guiding the Church

Ultimately, of course, our assurance that the Church will be faithful comes from Christ himself. Jesus said that the "gates of the netherworld" would not prevail against the Church (Matthew 16:18). The Church has interpreted this to mean that Christ would not allow the Church to be led astray in essential matters of faith or morals.

This is the basis for our doctrine of infallibility. The Second Vatican Council explains that the "body of the faithful as a whole, anointed as they are by the Holy One (cf. 1 John 2:20,27), cannot err in matters of belief....when, 'from the bishops down to the last member of the laity,' it shows universal agreement in matters of faith and morals" (SVC, *Church*, 12). The Council stated that bishops have this gift of infallibility when they, in agreement among themselves and with the pope, teach authentically on a matter of faith or morals which they concur is to be held conclusively, or when they so teach at an ecumenical council. The pope speaks infallibly when he speaks *ex cathedra*, as the leader of the whole Church, on a matter of faith or morals, expressly defining doctrine as a matter of faith (SVC, *Church*, 25).

The conditions under which a doctrine is said to be infallibly believed are very stringent, and infallible declarations are rare. An example would be the formal definition of Mary's Assumption by Pope Pius XII in 1950. Even then, Pius was expressing a belief which had long been accepted by the whole body of the faithful.

The Church's understanding of infallibility reflects the sacramental principle, for it maintains that the truth and wisdom of God may be found in human doctrinal statements. Infallibility assures us that God will not allow evil to lead the Church astray. It helps believers to distinguish what is essential from what is not. A clear understanding of infallibility and its limits may also be seen as a safeguard against the misuse of authority. Where there is no doctrine of infallibility, those in authority can easily claim the aura of infallibility, as when television evangelists "proclaim" that all

Catholics are doomed to hell eternally (a proclamation stronger than any pope has ever made!). Where there is no doctrine of infallibility, there is the temptation for religious leaders to claim infallibility in everything.

The Church's understanding of infallibility and its patterns of authority allow for a great deal of flexibility, and for diversity within unity. It is Church dogma that the Bible is inspired, but few particular verses of the Bible have been officially defined, and Catholic scholars differ widely in their interpretations of many biblical passages. We are one Catholic Church, but we come from many nations, cultures, and social classes. There are various rites of worship, different religious orders, and diverse approaches to spirituality. Many parishes, each with a distinct personality and usually under the leadership of a pastor, are joined to form a diocese under its bishop. Many dioceses, each with its distinct personality, are joined to form the universal Catholic Church, whose unity is signified by the office of the pope. (See SVC, *Church*, 23.)

The Church and Everyday Life

We have spoken of sharing the priesthood of Christ in its offices of teaching, governing, and sanctifying. This may sound very abstract, but it is as down-to-earth as parents teaching their children the Sign of the Cross, as members of a parish council discussing the construction of a new church, as friends attending Sunday Mass together every weekend. It means that Christ is as near to us as the folks who live next door or under our own roof.

The significance of this can hardly be overestimated. So many people think only of Jesus "in the sky," and expect Christ to minister to them in some miraculous way. Christ can work miracles, and he does, but most often Christ looks to the needs of his people through his Body on earth, the Church.

There's an old story which illustrates this point. Fred was sitting on the roof of his house watching flood waters creep up the shingles. Rescuers came by in a motorboat and urged him to climb in. "Don't worry about me," he said, "I trust in the Lord to save me." The waters continued to rise, and a policeman in a rowboat offered help, only to get the same answer. Finally, a helicopter hovered overhead and Fred was thrown a rope. "No thanks," called

Fred, "I trust only in the Lord." Fred could tread water only so long...and drowned. Ushered by an angel into the presence of God, he complained: "Lord, I trusted in you and you let me drown." "Don't blame me," said God, "I sent you two boats and a helicopter." We must realize that Christ comes to us through people, or we, too, will miss the boat!

On the night before he died, Jesus told his apostles, "Amen, amen, I say to you, whoever believes in me will do the works that I do, and will do greater ones than these, because I am going to the Father" (John 14:12). For almost two thousand years, believers have done the works of Jesus—teaching, governing, sanctifying, comforting, healing, and serving. We have it on Christ's authority that they have done greater works than he did in his mortal life on earth. Millions have been taught, governed, sanctified, comforted, healed, and served by the Church, which is, of course, Christ himself working through the members of his Body.

The Heart and Hands of Christ

If we are not aware of the fact that Christ comes to us through the Church, we can miss the many ways he enters our life. We can fail to be the heart and hands of Christ when he depends on us. An example...

Some time ago I was driving through Denver, Colorado, listening to a Christian talk show on the radio. A counselor was offering advice and spiritual guidance when a young lady called. "I'm very discouraged," she said. "I've heard ministers say that we should take our problems to Jesus and he will comfort and console us. I've done this, and I haven't experienced consolation. Many of my friends tell me the same thing, and this makes it hard for me to put my faith in Jesus."

The counselor first commended the caller for her honesty and stated that her experience was not unique, for in the Bible, Jeremiah complained about being abandoned by God (Jeremiah 15:10-21). The counselor recommended that the young lady speak to Jesus in prayer and let him know just how she felt.

This advice was good as far as it went, but it did not go far enough. The counselor might have asked the young lady, "Have you talked to your friends about your problems and have they helped you?" I suspect that the answer would have been yes. The counselor could then have pointed out that this is how Jesus gives us comfort and consolation—through people open to his Spirit. If the young lady had replied that she had no one to talk to, the counselor could have offered assistance; the situation was an opportunity for that counselor to be Christ for someone in need.

If we do not understand the sacramental principle, which means that Christ comes to us through the signs he has given us, through the people in our lives, and through events guided by divine Providence, we will fail to see how often Christ answers our prayers. We will fail to see how Christ depends upon us to allow him to answer the prayers of others.

When I was pastor of a small parish in Missouri, the school children frequently requested in their prayers at Mass "that God would send more priests and sisters to serve the Church." I told the children, "This is a prayer *you* must answer. Christ may be inviting some of you to be priests and sisters, inviting you to say yes to his call. He is certainly inviting all of us to be active members of his Church. If we don't say yes to him, our prayer won't be answered."

After the Ascension of Jesus into heaven, according to the Acts of the Apostles, two men in white garments appeared to the apostles and asked them, "Why are you standing there looking at the sky?" (Acts 1:11) The Ascension was really a sign that Jesus is God. God is everywhere, and Jesus would be not just "in the sky" but with them always, "until the end of the age" (Matthew 28:20).

Christ's Own Encore

After joining the human race, being born at Bethlehem, dying on the cross, and rising from the dead, what could Jesus Christ do for an encore?

He could, and did, continue his presence through his Church. He could, and did, send the Holy Spirit at Pentecost to empower and enlighten the apostles...and all those who were to follow in their footsteps as followers of Jesus.

We are challenged as Catholics to realize what a privilege it is to be among those followers, to be members of Christ's Body to continue his work in the world, to be part of Christ's own encore!

Questions for Discussion and Reflection

Have you thought of Jesus as being primarily "in the sky" or in the Church? Is this a case of "either/or" or "both/and"?

Can you think of prayers you've offered that Christ has answered through others? Can you think of occasions where perhaps you have been an answer to prayer?

A woman said to her spiritual advisor: "I worry about whether God really loves me. How can I know that I'm loved by God? I feel loved by my family and I have many friends, but I don't *feel* God's love." How would you respond to her?

What are some ways in which your parish is Christ to those in need? What are some ways your diocese and the universal Church are Christ to those in need?

Is it true to say that Christ has chosen to need us in order to continue his work in the world? Can each person manifest God's presence in a unique way? Can a single woman, a married couple, an elderly person, manifest God's presence in a way that Christ could not? Can *you* manifest God's presence in a way that no one else, even Jesus, can?

Activities

In the section, The Origins of the Church (page 33), there are Scripture citations (beginning with Acts 5:1-11) referring to failings in the early Church. Look up these passages and reflect on how they are found in today's Church. Pray for those who are failing, and ask God to help us all be Catholics after the mind of Jesus Christ.

Try to be an answer to someone's prayer today. Call a friend who might be lonely. Visit an elderly person in the nursing home. Be patient and kind to members of your family.

CHAPTER FOUR
Our Catholic Book, the Bible

T hink of a recent visit with a friend. You spent time together, you talked, you shook hands or hugged, you may have shared a meal or exchanged gifts. Friendship draws us to be with one another, to speak, and to share.

When Jesus lived his mortal life on earth, he loved to be with people. He spoke with them. He touched them in many ways. Jesus continues to be present to us through the Church. He continues to speak, especially through his Word in the Bible. He touches us, especially through the sacraments.

The Catholic Church has treasured the Bible as God's Word and the sacraments as actions of Christ. And the Church has always understood Bible and sacraments as flowing from the mystery of the Incarnation. They are both divine and human.

The Bible, Divine and Human

In the Bible, God addresses us. Jesus speaks to us the same words he spoke to the apostles. But the Bible did not drop from heaven. It was not dictated by God to human beings who simply acted as secretaries. Instead, God influenced people to use their own talents and ways of writing. God did this in such a way that the Bible is truly a work both divine and human, a work that exemplifies the sacramental principle. The written word, visible and tangible, makes present what is invisible and transcendent, the Word of God.

There is a paradox in the Bible, the reality that it is both human and divine. We should expect this in God's dealings with humans. We might also expect that some people would try to eliminate the paradox by focusing on either the human or the divine to the exclusion of the other.

Some have tried to explain the Bible as a merely human production. They have seen it as a literary work composed by human beings, to be studied and admired like other great works of literature. They regard the Bible as interesting and insightful, but in no way supernatural or divine.

Others have tried to explain the Bible as divine to such an extent that any human contribution is minimized. They say that God "dictated" the content of the Bible to its human authors. Or they seem to visualize the gift of a complete edition of the Bible from God to the first generation of Christians. Those who see the Bible in this way say that it must be taken in all its parts as absolute truth and that its meaning can be determined by the words alone. They hold that when someone reads the Bible today, God relays the divinely intended meaning directly to that individual. There is, they contend, no need for interpretation by a Church or for any other human intervention.

The Catholic Church rejects these errors and holds to the paradox that the Bible is at the same time divine and human. The official position of the Church was expressed by the Second Vatican Council: The books of the Bible "have God as their author and have been handed on as such to the Church herself." Human beings, making use of their own powers and abilities, are "true authors" of those same books (SVC, *Dogmatic Constitution on Divine Revelation,* 11). This divine and human authorship of the Bible was made possible through the process known as inspiration.

Inspiration

"All scripture is inspired by God and is useful for teaching, for refutation, for correction, and for training in righteousness" (2 Timothy 3:16; see also 2 Peter 1:20-21). In the Catholic understanding of inspiration, God guided the human authors of the biblical books to write in such a way that the books teach the religious truths intended by God. This does not mean that God merely dictated words to secretaries, but that God influenced the authors in such a way that the result is truly the Word of God and the work of human beings.

Exactly what the divine influence was seems to have varied. In some cases, it may have come in the form of miraculous events or supernatural visions (Isaiah 6). In others, it may have touched the authors without their realizing that God was working through them as they wrote. (See 2 Maccabees 2:19-32 and Luke 1:1-4.) What remained constant was the interaction between God and human beings which resulted in written works accepted by the Jewish and Christian communities as inspired by God.

Inspiration should be distinguished from revelation, which is the self-disclosure of God. Some things about God can be known through created realities in "natural" revelation. Other things are known only through supernatural revelation, the personal actions and words of God, especially in those of Jesus Christ (SVC, *Revelation*, 3–6). There is much revelation in the Bible, but many facts there did not have to be revealed because they were known by the authors through personal experience or scholarly research. Everything in the Bible is inspired because the entire Bible is the work of God and of human authors, but not everything in the Bible is revealed.

The interaction of God and human authors in the Bible brings up another issue, that of inerrancy, freedom from error. Those individuals who understand inspiration to mean "dictation" by God are likely to say that there can be no error of any kind in the Bible. The Catholic Church, which sees inspiration in terms of divine influence and human response, holds that "the books of Scripture must be acknowledged as teaching firmly, faithfully, and without error that truth which God wanted put into the sacred writings for the sake of our salvation" (SVC, *Revelation*, 11). Therefore, parts of the Bible which do not relate directly to human salvation need not be regarded as "without error."

Thus, the authors of Genesis probably understood the world as resting on pillars rather than as a globe spinning through space. These primitive notions were used to teach the spiritual truth that the world comes from God, rather than from nothing. The teaching that the world comes from God was inspired by God for the sake of our salvation. The notion that the world rests on pillars is not taught as such for our salvation; it merely "sets the stage" for the proclamation of religious truth.

Old Testament authors lacked the full revelation which came only with Jesus Christ. Some of them taught attitudes of hatred and revenge (Psalm 58, Psalm 137). Others questioned the reality of eternal life (Ecclesiastes 9). These attitudes and questions are recorded, not as facts inspired by God for our salvation, but as testimonials of what some Israelites believed as they struggled to respond to life's demands and to the wisdom of God. They help us to realize how much we need the full revelation of God's truth granted by Jesus Christ.

Such distinctions between inspiration, revelation, and inerrancy may seem complicated. Some Christians try to avoid complications by stating that there can be no error of any kind in the Bible, assuming either that it was dictated by God or that it was dropped from heaven. They say, for instance, that the story of creation in Genesis is meant to present an exact scientific account of how the world actually came to be. This is not the Catholic position. We see the Bible as the product of an infallible God and of fallible human beings. What God intended to teach for our salvation is without error. What human beings contributed is subject to human limitations.

Where do we find evidence for this position? In a study of the origins of the Bible. How can we tell what is infallibly taught? By interpreting the Bible with the guidance of the Church directed by the Holy Spirit.

The Origins of the Bible

The Bible came to us through a long, complex process involving God's interaction with many generations of human beings. A collection of books, it is divided into the Old Testament, written before Jesus Christ over a period of more than a thousand years, and the New Testament, written during the one hundred years after Christ's Resurrection. Much of the Old Testament, including the Pentateuch (the first five books of the Bible), was assembled from many ancient sources after the destruction of Jerusalem (586 B.C.). Other books regarded as sacred by the Jews were added as time went on, the last being the Book of Wisdom, written about 50 B.C.

At the time of Christ, there were two collections of Old Testament books. One of these collections, the Palestinian, was written in Hebrew. The other, the Alexandrian (Septuagint), included a Greek translation of the Hebrew books and a number of books written in Greek. The Palestinian and Alexandrian collections were honored by different Jewish communities, but because the New Testament authors wrote in Greek, they tended to use the Alexandrian collection, and it soon became the accepted "Old Testament" of the Christian community. The Palestinian collection was later chosen by a group of Jewish scholars as their sacred book about A.D. 100, partially in reaction to the Christian use of the Alexandrian collection.

By A.D. 125, many writings about Jesus, including all of those now found in the New Testament, were being circulated among Christians. Some of the writings were regarded as authoritative because of their apostolic origins and doctrinal content. Some were rejected because they contained false teachings. Gradually, the Christian community began to regard certain writings as inspired by God. By the end of the fourth century, there was general consensus that the Christian Bible should contain the forty-six books of the Alexandrian Old Testament and the twenty-seven books of the New Testament now found in the Catholic Bible. Such consensus was reflected in lists of biblical books drawn up in the Church councils of Hippo in A.D. 393 and of Carthage in A.D. 397.

There was little disagreement among Christians until the sixteenth century, when Protestants rejected the Alexandrian (Christian) list of Old Testament books in favor of the Palestinian (Jewish) list. At this time, Martin Luther relegated Hebrews, James, Jude, and Revelation to a secondary position in the New Testament; however, other Protestants maintained the traditional New Testament list, and it soon prevailed.

In 1546 the Council of Trent defined the Alexandrian as the official list of Old Testament books for Catholics and reaffirmed the traditional list of New Testament books. As a result, while Catholics and Protestants today share the same New Testament of twenty-seven books, the Protestant Old Testament contains seven fewer books than the Catholic: Tobit, Judith, First and Second Maccabees, Wisdom, Sirach (sometimes called Ecclesiasticus), and Baruch (plus additions to Esther and Daniel). These are placed in some Protestant Bibles as the "Apocrypha" ("hidden books").

The books of the Bible, then, came from many authors who acted under God's inspiration. Those books were designated by the Christian community and by councils of Catholic bishops as divinely inspired. Both the inspiration and the designation involved many human beings acting over a long period of time. The Bible clearly was not dropped from heaven or merely dictated to secretaries who neatly fitted their books into a preexisting Bible.

Interpreting the Bible

The Bible is the result of complex interaction between God and human beings. It was written in languages foreign to us (Hebrew, Greek, and Aramaic) and has had to be translated into modern English. It came from cultures far different from ours. It was written over a long period of time. It contains many different kinds of literary forms (styles of writing), including history, prophecy, poetry, law, proverbs (wise sayings), myths (fictional stories or actual events which explain ultimate reality), legends (popular unverifiable stories handed down from the past, often conveying a moral), fables (fictitious stories, often with animal characters, that teach a lesson), and parables (simple stories that illustrate a moral or a religious lesson).

Given all these circumstances, and given the content of the Bible, which is the story of God's interaction with human beings, we should expect that reading the Bible and understanding its message would require serious study, reflection, and interpretation. And of course it does.

There are two basic approaches to interpreting the Bible. The "fundamentalist" method begins with the notion that God simply dictated the Bible to its human authors. It tends to ignore the historical origins of the Bible. It holds that the words of the Bible must be taken only at face value.

The contextual method, the one taught at the Second Vatican Council, states that we must have the context of any given passage to understand it properly. This approach requires that we discover the original intent of the authors by analyzing their purpose in writing, as well as their times, culture, language and other circumstances.

For example, fundamentalists would see the Book of Genesis as modern history or as a science textbook. If the words of Genesis 1, taken at face value, say that the world was created in six days and that God rested on the seventh, this must be how it happened. The contextual approach would lead us to study when, where, why, and by whom the book was written and so arrive at the conclusion that Genesis 1 teaches religious truths, not precise scientific data.

It should be noted that in both cases interpretation of the Book of Genesis is required. Fundamentalists interpret the book when they say readers must believe that God created everything in six days. Contextualists interpret it when they say Genesis was written to teach religious truth. It is simply impossible to take all biblical passages at face value. Psalm 144:1 says of God, "Blessed be the LORD, my rock." This obviously does not mean that God is solid mineral matter. The passage requires interpretation. So does nearly every passage of the Bible. The real issue is what principles will be used in interpreting the Bible.

Catholic Principles for Interpreting the Bible

Fundamentalists tend to ignore the sacramental principle in that they emphasize the divine authorship of the biblical books and minimize the human authorship. They tend also to interpret the Bible according to the subjective principles of individual preachers or according to their own "personal" interpretation.

Catholics are encouraged to interpret the Bible with due attention to the sacramental principle, realizing that God's inspiration does not negate the contribution of the human authors. Catholics are advised to interpret the Bible according to objective principles recommended by Bible scholars and endorsed by the Church. Acknowledging the importance of the Church is itself related to the sacramental principle, for it recognizes that God guides us most often not by "mystical experiences from on high," but by the down-to-earth common sense of the Church, the Body of Christ.

The first principle of Catholic interpretation given us through the Church is that we, "in order to see clearly what God wanted to communicate to us, should carefully investigate what meaning the sacred writers really intended, and what God wanted to manifest by means of their words" (SVC, *Revelation*, 12). We must go back to the time, place, way of life, mode of thinking, and manners of expression of the biblical authors. "For the correct understanding of what the sacred author wanted to assert, due attention must be paid to the customary and characteristic styles of perceiving, speaking, and narrating which prevailed at the time of the sacred writer" (SVC, *Revelation*, 12).

A second important principle is that we must interpret a given passage in light of the other passages which relate to it. An example of this is Matthew 26:26-28, where Jesus said over the bread and wine: "This is my body....This is my blood." Curiously enough, many fundamentalists refuse to take this passage literally. But Catholics interpret it in the light of John 6, where Jesus proclaims himself to be the bread of life. When Jesus said that we must eat his flesh and drink his blood, many of his hearers abandoned him. Jesus did not call them back and tell them, "You misunderstood. I only meant that in a symbolic way." What he was asking them to believe was hard to accept, and when they refused, Jesus sadly let them go. Other passages, such as 1 Corinthians 11:27, also point to the Real Presence of Jesus under the appearances of the bread and wine. Catholics believe, then, that Jesus is truly present in the Eucharist.

Biblical authors often accentuate one point of an issue, without denying all the other dimensions of that issue. Thus, in Galatians 3:1-9, Paul emphasizes that justification comes through faith in Christ rather than through observance of the Jewish law. By saying this, Paul is not advising disobedience to all laws. He is not denying the importance of good works, for in Galatians 5–6 he emphasizes them as the way to "inherit the kingdom of God." Faith is essential, but so are good works. It is possible, by picking and choosing certain parts of the Bible to the exclusion of others, to argue almost any position! An honest examination of all passages relating to any given subject may be more difficult than picking and choosing, but it is more likely to arrive at the truth.

A third principle, closely related to the second, is that "serious attention must be given to the content and unity of the whole of Scripture, if the meaning of the sacred texts is to be correctly brought to light" (SVC, *Revelation*, 12). In particular, the Old Testament ought to be read and interpreted in the light of the New. There are passages in the Old Testament, like Ecclesiastes 9:4-6, which question the reality of eternal life. Such questioning was put to rest by the teaching of Jesus, and we understand the imperfect theology of the Old Testament as an indication of humanity's need for the full revelation of God's truth given by Jesus Christ.

The Bible: A Catholic Book

Sometimes Catholics are criticized for belonging to a Church that is not biblical. Such criticism comes from ignorance of history and of the Catholic Church's reverence for the Bible. In fact, it is not an exaggeration to call the Bible a "Catholic" book. This is not to deny it to anyone else. But it does recognize the simple fact that if it were not for the Catholic Church, there would be no Bible.

The original Christian Bible was formed in communities of believers presided over by Catholic bishops and finalized into a collection through the decisions of councils of Catholic bishops. The Bible was preserved and handed down through the centuries by the Catholic Church. Before the invention of the printing press, Catholic monks and nuns copied each letter of every word of the Bible by hand. Many of these handwritten manuscripts survive today, testimonials to the love and artistic skill of those who created them.

For two thousand years, the Bible has been read daily at Catholic celebrations of the Eucharist. In catacombs, in private homes, and in cathedrals God's Word has been proclaimed to Catholics, a continuing witness to the Church's reverence for the Bible. The Catholic *Lectionary*, a book of Scripture readings following a three-year cycle for Sundays and a two-year cycle for weekdays, was the model for the *Common Lectionary* used in many Protestant churches.

The Catholic Church encourages its members to read the Bible. The bishops of Vatican II wrote:

"This sacred Synod earnestly and specifically urges all the Christian faithful...to learn by frequent reading of the divine Scriptures the 'excelling knowledge of Jesus Christ' (Philippians 3:8). 'For ignorance of the Scriptures is ignorance of Christ.' Therefore, they should gladly put themselves in touch with the sacred text itself, whether it be through the liturgy, rich in the divine word, or through devotional reading, or through instructions suitable for the purpose....And let them remember that prayer should accompany the reading of sacred Scripture, so that God and man may talk together; for 'we speak to Him when we pray; we hear Him when we read the divine sayings'" (SVC, *Revelation*, 25).

The Bible: We and God "Talk Together"

The passage just quoted from the Second Vatican Council emphasizes an important fact about our Catholic approach to the Bible. Through the Bible, we "talk together" with God. The Bible is a sacramental sign through which God tells us of divine love, wisdom, forgiveness, compassion, and guidance. The Bible is a sacramental sign allowing us to speak to God in the same words used by Jesus Christ and by great men and women of our Jewish-Christian family.

This is possible because God is not limited by space and time. God's knowledge of and love for us are infinite. When we pick up the Bible, God is instantly aware of it. As we read the words of the Bible, God is present, addressing those words to us in our particular situation and circumstances.

This is the most significant difference between the Bible and other books. When we read any other book, we may be informed or entertained by its contents; its author, however, is not conscious of us as we read. But when we pick up the Bible, we "dial God's number." God says "Hello," and "redirects" the words of the Bible to our particular situation and needs.

People use various techniques to remind themselves of this reality. Some, when preparing to read the Bible privately, picture themselves as "dialing God's number," actually engaging God in a telephone conversation. Some, when hearing the Bible proclaimed at Sunday Mass or other acts of worship, visualize Jesus himself standing at the lectern. These techniques use the imagination, but there is a sacramental reality behind the images. God really does talk with us when we read the Bible. Christ is speaking through the lector at church, for that lector is part of the Body of Christ.

In order for us to receive the full benefit of the words of Scripture, we should have an intelligent grasp of the essential requirements for reading the Bible. We should be familiar with the contents of the Bible so that we can locate passages which are especially relevant to our needs.

Above all, we should, as the Second Vatican Council recommends, accompany Bible reading with prayer. We should ask God to help us become more conscious of the fact that through the Bible we "talk together" with the Father, Son, and Holy Spirit.

When we are aware of the Bible as a sacrament of conversation with God, then God can speak to us here and now. Words that we have read many times in the past may touch us with new power when we are grieving at the death of a loved one, when we are confused and don't know where to turn, when we are looking for the answers to any of life's questions.

"Indeed, the word of God is living and effective...and able to discern reflections and thoughts of the heart" (Hebrews 4:12). When we are discouraged, Jesus says to us, "Come to me, all you who labor and are burdened, and I will give you rest" (Matthew 11:28). When we are fearful, Jesus tells us, "Peace be with you" (John 20:19). When we are lonely, Jesus assures us, "I am with you always" (Matthew 28:20).

"Talking together with God" implies that we do more than just hear God's Word. We also respond. We respond in *prayer*: We read God's words, then talk to God as we would to any friend. We respond through our *life choices:* We read until we come to a phrase that challenges us, then make a decision based on what God has spoken to us.

No other book allows us to "talk together" with God in this way. As we Catholics grow in our appreciation of the Bible, we will learn not only to read the Bible but to love it as our Book. We will then be ready to answer a question God may ask at the final judgment: "How did you like my book?"

As Catholics, we ought to have the right answer. God's book, the Bible, is a part of our heritage. We are privileged to read it and to love it as members of a community which formed and preserved the Bible, and which understands it as God's Word "incarnate," divine and human, as Jesus speaking to us today.

Questions for Discussion and Reflection

Can you explain in your own words the meaning of inspiration, revelation, and inerrancy? How are they different? How are they related?

Sometimes Catholics are asked, "Why did you Catholics add seven books to the Old Testament?" What is wrong with this question? What is a good response to it?

Can you explain in your own words the three principles of Catholic Bible interpretation given in the text? In what ways may the Bible be called a Catholic book?

Have you ever thought of opening the Bible as initiating a conversation with God? How does God speak to you? How do you respond to God?

Activities

Find a quiet place. Take your Bible, look up a favorite passage, and enjoy "talking together" with God.

CHAPTER FIVE
Sacred Tradition–Christ Teaches Through His Church

Every Fourth of July, Den, Kathy, and their family invite friends for a backyard barbecue and swim party. Adults and children spend a leisurely afternoon splashing in the pool, playing lawn games, and enjoying hot dogs and hamburgers off the grill. After dark, smaller children play with sparklers under the watchful supervision of parents, and the celebration ends with a mini-fireworks display conducted by the teenagers.

When December rolls around, David, Pat and their children set up a crib in the family room; each day, after the evening meal, they say a short prayer together, and one of the children places a lamb, shepherd, or angel near the crib. On Christmas Eve, the children put Mary, Joseph, and the baby Jesus in the crib, and the whole family sings "O Little Town of Bethlehem."

Families have "traditions," customs and time-honored ways of doing things. The Catholic Church has "traditions" in local parishes and throughout the world. Some parishes, for example, have a May crowning. Eighth grade girls place a wreath of flowers on a statue of the Blessed Virgin, while the congregation sings traditional Marian hymns. Worldwide, the Catholic Church has customary times when collections are taken up to aid the poor and needy.

The Catholic Church also has sacred Tradition. By this is meant, not just customs and common practices, but truth revealed by God and handed on from the apostles in the official teaching of the Church. "Now what was handed on by the apostles includes everything which contributes to the holiness of life and the increase in faith of the People of God; and so the Church, in her teaching, life, and worship perpetuates and hands on to all generations all that she herself is, all that she believes" (SVC, *Revelation*, 8). Sacred Tradition is expressed most clearly in creeds, liturgical worship, decisions of councils, infallible statements by the pope, the Church's interpretation of the Bible, and the consistent belief of the faithful through the centuries.

Natural Revelation

The Catholic understanding of sacred Tradition is rooted in the sacramental principle, in our realization that God deals with human beings in ways we can see, touch, and feel. We believe that divine revelation is not limited to truths found in the Bible, for some truths about God have been available to human beings for as long as people have walked the face of this earth.

All creation reveals the Creator to us: "The heavens declare the glory of God; the sky proclaims its builder's craft" (Psalm 19:2). From the beginning, human beings have gazed at the sun, moon, and stars, and have seen them as masterpieces revealing the power and splendor of their Creator. Philosophers have reasoned that the universe, which exists without a sufficient reason in itself, must have a sufficient reason outside itself, a Creator, namely God. Poets have sung that the world is full of the grandeur of God.

And so Saint Paul taught: "Ever since the creation of the world, his [God's] invisible attributes of eternal power and divinity have been able to be understood and perceived in what he has made" (Romans 1:20). The Second Vatican Council stated: "God, who through the Word creates all things...and keeps them in existence, gives men an enduring witness to Himself in created realities..." (SVC, *Revelation*, 3).

The truths about God, such as God's existence, which are known through nature and history, are called "natural revelation." The reality of such revelation has been a standard principle of Catholic theology, even when others have rejected it. It shows our Catholic belief that God is present in the world, disclosing God's very Self in and through creation, and that people, things, and events teach us about God and lead us to God. It opens us up to the reality that God's revelation is made available to us in many ways.

Supernatural Revelation

God has not been content to leave human beings to their own resources in seeking knowledge about their Creator and the origin and purpose of their lives. Rather, God has revealed truth by reaching across the barriers of space and time to speak to humanity in miraculous ways, in ways "above nature," in supernatural revelation.

The family of Abraham and Sarah, those people ultimately known as the Jews, listened and responded to God's invitation to intimacy and friendship. Gradually, through centuries of relationship with God, they learned that there was one God, that God had created all things, that God loved people and wanted them to freely follow God's laws, especially those guidelines known as the Ten Commandments.

As time went on, however, many of the Jews ignored the Lord's teaching and disobeyed God's commandments. They suffered one disaster after another. Eventually, some of them, learning from their mistakes and from God's revelation, came to the conclusion that only God could save them. They began to look for a Savior from God, a Messiah, who would lead them to the happiness and fulfillment they longed for.

That Messiah surpassed their expectations to an infinite degree, for he was Jesus Christ, the Word of God made flesh (John 1). Jesus spoke the words of God and revealed the face of God (John 14:9). He was the perfect revelation from God; in Jesus, God "spoke to us through a son, whom he made heir of all things and through whom he created the universe" (Hebrews 1:2).

Jesus, by his teaching, revealed God as Father, Son, and Holy Spirit. He assured us of God's love and of God's willingness to forgive our sins. He affirmed the reality of life after death. He explained God's plan for us, summed up in the great commandments of love of God and neighbor. He disclosed his intention to remain in the world for all time through the Church he formed of his followers.

Jesus revealed truth not only by his words but by his actions. He showed love and compassion to all, even to sinners. He healed the sick and raised the dead. He conquered death by accepting death on the cross and rising to new life. He sent the Holy Spirit to his followers to form them into a Church and to inspire them to proclaim the Good News of his life, death, and resurrection.

The Transmission of Supernatural Revelation

The apostles and early followers of Jesus fulfilled his mandate to bring God's revelation to the world by preaching and by example. Some of them, under the inspiration of the Holy Spirit, committed their proclamation of Christ to writing. In time, as we have seen, the Church recognized twenty-seven writings about Jesus as divinely inspired. The Church also named forty-six books of the Old Testament as inspired by God. In this way, much of the message of salvation was committed to writing and given to the world (SVC, *Revelation*, 7).

"But in order to keep the gospel forever whole and alive within the Church, the apostles left bishops as their successors, 'handing over their own teaching role' to them" (SVC, *Revelation*, 7). The apostles handed on both their message and their ministry. Thus, the preaching of the apostles was "to be preserved by a continuous succession of preachers until the end of time" (SVC, *Revelation*, 8).

Revelation, Scripture, and Tradition

The idea that God's supernatural revelation is transmitted in two ways, through sacred Scripture and through sacred Tradition, has always been accepted by the Catholic Church. It is rejected by many other churches, especially those which interpret the Bible in a fundamentalist way. Often, people who belong to such churches attack Catholics because we believe "things that are not found in the Bible." They state that we can believe "only what the Bible says."

Why do Catholics believe that God has revealed truths which are to be "handed on" through sacred Tradition? There are many reasons. The first is that we believe in the sacramental principle! We believe that God is constantly interacting with people. God did not simply drop a Bible from the sky and then stop communicating with people. God continues to speak to us through the Word, Jesus

Christ (John 1:1), who continues to speak through his Church. Jesus promised to send the Holy Spirit to lead the Church to the truth: "I have much more to tell you....But when he comes, the Spirit of truth, he will guide you to all truth" (John 16:13). God's Word, then, is addressed to the world through the teaching of the apostles and their successors, guided by the Holy Spirit.

Second, the Church existed for a long time without the Bible as we know it. No New Testament works existed until at least twenty years after Christ's Resurrection, and the last book of the New Testament was written about seventy years after the Resurrection. If all revelation had to be found in the Bible, the early Church would have had little to teach.

Third, Church councils made the decisions about which books should be accepted into the Bible. Without the living teaching authority of the Church, without sacred Tradition, there would be no Bible, for there would have been no way to determine which books belonged in the Bible and which did not. This is another way of saying that the Church produced the Bible. The Bible did not produce the Church. Ask the question, "What is the pillar and foundation of truth?" Many Christians will answer, "The Bible, of course." But that's not what the Bible says! The Bible states that the *Church* is "the pillar and foundation of truth" (1 Timothy 3:15).

Fourth, the Bible makes it clear that all of God's truth is not found in sacred Scripture. John's Gospel closes with the statement: "There are also many other things that Jesus did, but if these were to be described individually, I do not think the whole world would contain the books that would be written" (John 21:25).

Fifth, the Bible itself indicates that God's truth would be "handed on" by preaching, as well as by the written word. Jesus said to his disciples, "Whoever listens to you listens to me" (Luke 10:16), thus showing that God's revelation would be brought to the world through the teaching of the apostles. The New Testament reports this mandate of Paul to Timothy: "And what you heard from me through many witnesses entrust to faithful people who will have the ability to teach others" (2 Timothy 2:2).

Sixth, Scripture explicitly acknowledges traditions passed on by the leaders of the Church and not found in the Bible. Saint Paul wrote to the Thessalonians, and to us: "...stand firm and hold fast to the traditions that you were taught, either by an oral statement or by a letter of ours" (2 Thessalonians 2:15).

Finally, there is no passage in the Bible which says that the Bible is the only source of divine revelation. Therefore, anyone who asserts that the Bible is the only source of revelation is claiming something that is not in the Bible. Anyone who says we must believe only what we find in the Bible is asking us to believe something that is not in the Bible!

Sacred Tradition and Sacred Scripture

Tradition means "handing on," and sacred Tradition includes the way the Church has handed on the Bible. We have already seen that it was the Church, the community of believers, which received the Scriptures from God and which has handed them on by preserving them, copying them, and distributing them.

Sacred Tradition also helps Catholics understand the sacred Scriptures. Many passages in the Bible require some interpretation. The Catholic Church offers guidance to the faithful by presenting general principles of interpretation of the Bible. (See SVC, *Revelation*, 11–13.) The Church has not made formal dogmatic statements about the specific meaning of most Scripture passages. Those passages, however, related to basic Catholic doctrines like the Trinity, the Incarnation, and Christ's Real Presence in the Eucharist have been officially interpreted by Church councils or by popes under the guidance of the Holy Spirit. Such passages show the interaction of Scripture and sacred Tradition within the Catholic Church and illustrate how both Scripture and sacred Tradition help Catholics understand God's revelation.

Sacred Tradition has not only helped the Church discover and interpret the Bible. Sacred Tradition has brought Catholics to a more complete grasp of God's truth than could be attained from the Bible alone. As a matter of fact, most Catholic dogmas (the foundational principles which all Catholics must believe) are found explicitly in the Bible. Some, like the doctrines of the Immaculate Conception and Assumption of Mary, are not found explicitly, but they have been revealed by God to the Church. Since such doctrines come from the same Source of truth as does the Bible, they cannot contradict the Bible and they are in harmony with the Bible. Thus, the Second Vatican Council wrote that the Church "has always regarded the Scriptures together with sacred tradition as the supreme rule of faith, and will ever do so" (SVC, *Revelation*, 21).

Finally, sacred Tradition and the official teaching office of the Church also help Catholics apply Bible teachings to modern problems. An example of this is the issue of abortion. Some Christians argue that abortion is morally acceptable, and state that abortion is not forbidden in the Bible. Catholics (and many other Christians) believe that abortion is forbidden by the commandment, "You shall not kill" (Exodus 20:13). The official teachers of the Church, the pope and bishops, begin with the Bible pronouncement, "You shall not kill." They see that the traditional teaching of the Church has forbidden the killing of unborn children. They look to the findings of modern medical science, which show clearly that the unborn child is not merely a "blob of tissue" but a human being. Tradition and the official teachers of the Church clarify for Catholics what the Bible mandates in a matter that is crucial to the moral standards of every individual and of society.

The Deposit of Faith and Development of Doctrine

The Catholic Church believes that there can be "no further new public revelation," for in Jesus Christ, "the full revelation of the supreme God is brought to completion" (SVC, *Revelation*, 4, 7). The truths revealed by Christ are contained in Tradition and sacred Scripture, forming "one sacred deposit of the word of God, which is committed to the Church" (SVC, *Revelation*, 10). In other words, the basic content of our faith is complete, and the Church believes that God revealed all the truths necessary for our salvation through Jesus Christ.

However, "there is a growth in the understanding of the realities and the words which have been handed down" in Scripture and sacred Tradition (SVC, *Revelation*, 8). In this sense, there can be a development of doctrine as believers contemplate God's revelation and as the ministers of the Church preach God's Word. "For, as the centuries succeed one another, the Church constantly moves forward toward the fullness of divine truth until the words of God reach their complete fulfillment in her" (SVC, *Revelation*, 8).

This happens because God is constantly interacting with the human race. Christ speaks to us through the Church and guides us through the Holy Spirit, and as a result we grow in understanding of the Scriptures and of sacred Tradition. For example, we have a more thorough understanding of the role of Mary in God's plan for our salvation than the early Church could have had. This understanding is beautifully expressed in the final chapter of the Second Vatican Council's *Dogmatic Constitution on the Church,* entitled "The Role of the Blessed Virgin Mary, Mother of God, in the Mystery of Christ and the Church." The *Constitution* itself is the result of twenty centuries of reflection by the Church on the truths contained in sacred Scriptures and sacred Tradition.

Attentiveness to Divine Revelation

Being Catholic means being open to God's truth as it is revealed in nature, in the Bible, and in sacred Tradition. As those who believe in the sacramental principle, we ought to see all the beauty and majesty of nature as gifts of God to us, as "valentines" sent to us by our Creator. The heavens declare the glory of God, and so do the hills and valleys, the forests and flowers, the oceans and streams, and all the finned, feathered, and furred creatures that share the planet with us. The life and beauty all around us are "natural revelation," signs of God's love and power and majesty. To be aware of this truth is to open ourselves to the privilege of abiding in the presence of God, for in God "we live and move and have our being" (Acts 17:28).

As Catholics, we are privileged to possess and read the Bible in the light of our Church's sacred Tradition. The more we know of our creeds, liturgical worship, formal teachings by popes and councils of bishops, and the consistent belief of the faithful through the centuries, the better we will understand those truths found explicitly and implicitly in the Bible. These truths of supernatural revelation enable us, as the Second Vatican Council points out, to know with ease what might be known from natural revelation only with difficulty (SVC, *Revelation*, 6).

Since natural and supernatural revelation come from one Source, God, there can be no contradiction between scientific truth and revealed truth. Apparent conflicts can occur, however, if theologians make the mistake of using the Bible as a science book, or if scientists make the mistake of confusing science and religion. Thus, Church leaders of the seventeenth century made serious mistakes in their dispute with Galileo because they used the Bible as an astronomy textbook. Since then, by being open to scientific discoveries and to the guidance of the Holy Spirit, Church officials have learned that the Bible was never intended to give a schematic diagram of the universe or a blueprint for how it functions.

Unfortunately, some people today still repeat the mistakes of those seventeenth-century theologians. They claim that the accounts of Genesis 1–3 must be taken at face value. They try to judge the age of the universe from dates given in the Bible, and come up with conclusions that seem incredible to anyone aware of modern scientific studies. When presented with evidence showing that the universe is billions of years old, for example, they state that God created the universe with "signs of age" built in to test our faith!

Some scientists err in the opposite direction by trying to show that evidence for the big bang theory of the origin of the universe argues against the existence of a Creator. They contend that evolutionary processes in the development of life on earth show that belief in God is unnecessary. They draw assumptions about theology from scientific data, thus making the mistake of using science books as Bibles, which is as misleading as using the Bible as a science book.

The Catholic Church teaches that both science and religion can teach the truth, and that true science and true religion are never in conflict. Science deals with what is measurable and observable, the "how" of created things. Religion studies divine realities, the "why" of all that exists, of what cannot be subjected to measurement because God is beyond space and time.

The Catholic Church believes that all truth, whether drawn from science or revealed by God, can light our way to God. Following the sacramental principle, that God is present in the world disclosing God's very Self in and through creation, Catholics are confident that the more we know about our universe, the more we are open to the greatness of God. We are equally confident that the truths God has revealed can never mislead us, and that guided by them, we can move confidently toward our eternal destiny, "eternal life through Jesus Christ our Lord" (Romans 5:21).

God invites us not only to learn the truth but also to share in the work of spreading the gospel. As Catholics, we revere God's natural revelation. We treasure God's supernatural revelation—

sacred Scripture and sacred Tradition, the result of Jesus' presence in his Church and his promise of the Spirit. We are privileged, as members of Christ's Body to "hand on," under the guidance of the Holy Spirit, that which has been handed on to us.

Questions for Discussion and Reflection

Consider this reflection on natural revelation (with apologies to Elizabeth Barrett Browning!): "The world's afire with the glory of God, and every bush aflame with God's presence. But only those with eyes of faith take off their shoes and see the Lord. The rest stand around and pick blackberries."

What does this reflection mean to you? What event in the Bible is alluded to?

Explain in your own words the meaning of the following terms: tradition; sacred Tradition; natural revelation; supernatural revelation.

Activities

Go for a walk, and notice the beauty of nature. Be conscious of the sights, sounds, and scents all around you. Think of all that you notice as God's gift to you, telling you something about God's creative power and love for you. Talk to God in your own words, and thank God for the beauty of creation.

In the first five chapters of this book, you have read many quotations from the Second Vatican Council. Read over some of them and consider the words as God's message spoken to you by the official teachers of the Church. Thank God for guiding the Church through the Holy Spirit.

CHAPTER SIX
Our Catholic Sacraments

T ry to picture a world without handshakes or hugs, birthday cakes or flowers, school jackets or wedding rings. Such a world might be suitable for angels, but not for human beings made of flesh and blood. Catholics have never been able to imagine a Church without flesh-and-blood signs. Catholics have always believed that Christ is truly present in the signs we call sacraments and that he touches us through them.

The Sacraments, Signs from Christ

The classic definition of sacraments explains them as "outward signs instituted by Christ to give grace." We may also define sacraments as signs from Christ by which he comes to us and gives us his life and love. Both definitions show our Catholic belief that sacraments find their origin in Jesus Christ and therefore have been part of the Church's life from the beginning. An organized theology of the sacraments was developed gradually under the guidance of the Holy Spirit, and by the thirteenth century the Church recognized seven special signs as sacraments given by Christ. The Council of Trent declared as dogma that these are Baptism, Confirmation, Eucharist, Penance, Matrimony, Holy Orders, and Anointing of the Sick.

In Chapter Two, we saw that Jesus himself is a sacrament, the sign who made God known to humanity and made it possible for humanity to touch God. Christ's life, ministry, and teaching were "sacramental" in nature, and laid the foundation for the Church's ministry of the seven sacraments, each of which can be found in the New Testament.

These seven sacraments are signs composed of words, actions, and things which symbolize spiritual realities. And because they are gifts to the Church from Christ himself, they are more than symbols. They bring about for people of faith the effects they symbolize. The water of Baptism, for example, symbolizes cleansing and new life, and because Jesus is present at Baptism, the sacrament actually cleanses a person from sin and gives the new life of God's grace.

Baptism

The Jewish people of Jesus' time practiced ceremonial washings (John 2:6). Jesus' cousin, John the Baptist, announced the coming of the Messiah to the Jews and invited them to acknowledge their sinfulness and need for repentance by baptism (washing) in the Jordan River. Though Jesus was sinless, he asked John to baptize him, perhaps to show his oneness with humanity (Matthew 3:1-17). Jewish ceremonial washings and John's baptism were merely symbolic, but they provided a framework for the apostles to understand Jesus' post-Resurrection mandate: "Go, therefore, and make disciples of all nations, baptizing them in the name of the Father, and of the Son, and of the holy Spirit" (Matthew 28:19).

On the first Pentecost, Peter said to the crowds, who were moved by his sermon on Christ's death and resurrection, "Repent and be baptized, every one of you, in the name of Jesus Christ for the forgiveness of your sins; and you will receive the gift of the holy Spirit" (Acts 2:38). For the apostles, the Baptism given them by Christ was more than a symbol. It took away the sins of those who repented, and it conferred God's Holy Spirit.

Saint Paul explained Baptism as a participation in the death and resurrection of Jesus. "We were indeed buried with him through baptism into death, so that, just as Christ was raised from the dead by the glory of the Father, we too might live in newness of life. For if we have grown into union with him through a death like his, we shall also be united with him in the resurrection" (Romans 6:4-5).

Baptism confers "newness of life" on this earth, as well as the promise of eternal life.

We Catholics, then, see Baptism as something more than an event in our past. Baptism gives us an ongoing relationship with Jesus Christ, joining us and our mortal existence to the eternal life of Christ. Baptism does not cover up our sins. It takes them away and offers union with Christ, so that everything we do can be done "for the glory of God" (1 Corinthians 10:31). Baptism makes our lives a sacrament, and imparts to our finite, physical actions an infinite, spiritual dimension.

Confirmation

Christ revealed that God is Father, Son, and Holy Spirit. He spoke of God in concrete, rather than abstract, terms. We can easily identify with the concept of God as Father, especially since Jesus painted such a vivid picture of God as a forgiving parent (Luke 15:11-32). We can envision God as Son, since the Son became one of us in Jesus Christ. We may find it more difficult to relate to God the Holy Spirit.

Jesus helps us, however, because he used clear, sacramental images to indicate the presence and power of the Holy Spirit. When Jesus was baptized in the Jordan River, the Holy Spirit descended on him in the form of a dove (Matthew 3:16-17). Jesus called the Holy Spirit our "Advocate," our Helper who guides us and favors our cause (John 14:15-18; 16:7-14). On Pentecost, Jesus sent the Holy Spirit upon the apostles in the form of wind and fire, symbolizing the power of God's strength and love (Acts 2:1-4). As wind moves ships across the ocean, so the Holy Spirit moved the apostles to bring the gospel to the world. As fire warms and gives light, so the Holy Spirit warmed the hearts of the apostles with God's love and enlightened their minds with God's wisdom.

The Catholic Church believes that Jesus, who spoke of the Spirit in such vivid terms and sent the Spirit in sacramental signs, continues to send the Holy Spirit upon his Church through the sacrament of Confirmation. In the New Testament, the sending of the Holy Spirit was usually associated with Baptism. For example, Peter told his hearers on Pentecost, "Repent and be baptized...and you will receive the gift of the holy Spirit" (Acts 2:38). But the New Testament also describes occasions when the Spirit was sent after Baptism. The people of Samaria were evangelized and baptized by Philip, the deacon. When news of this reached Jerusalem, the apostles "sent them Peter and John, who went down and prayed for them, that they might receive the holy Spirit, for it had not yet fallen upon any of them; they had only been baptized in the name of the Lord Jesus. Then they laid hands on them and they received the holy Spirit" (Acts 8:14-17; see Acts 19). Such passages provided a scriptural basis for the celebration of Confirmation, a sacramental bestowal of the Holy Spirit apart from Baptism. When infant Baptism became common among Catholics, Confirmation was usually conferred later, when the baptized had at least reached the age of reason.

After centuries of celebrating Confirmation and reflecting on its meaning, the Church sees this sacrament as an action of Christ by which he gives the Holy Spirit to us for strength, service, and evangelization. This sacrament joins the human and the divine, as the Holy Spirit dwells within us as our Advocate and Helper. When we are fully open to the love and grace of the Holy Spirit, the Spirit's presence gives us new potential and power in our efforts to imitate Christ. Traditionally, the effects of the Holy Spirit's presence have been called the *gifts* of the Spirit: wisdom, understanding, counsel, knowledge, courage, reverence, and piety (Isaiah 11:2). The results of the Holy Spirit's friendship are called the *fruits* of the Spirit: love, joy, peace, patience, kindness, generosity, faith, mildness, and chastity (Galatians 5:22-23). When such gifts and fruits are expressed in our words and actions, the presence of the Holy Spirit is "sacramentalized," made visible in our lives today.

Eucharist

For human beings, meals do more than feed the body. Meals are times for sharing friendship and for celebration. The Jewish people saw certain kinds of meals as expressing their special relationship to God and to one another. Their annual Passover meal, for example, recalled how they had been led out of slavery and formed into God's people. The sacrifice of a lamb and the eating of its flesh recalled all that God had done for them.

On the night before he died, Jesus shared a Passover meal with his apostles. He called them his friends and indicated that he would give his life for them, the greatest possible act of love (John 15:13-14). "Then he took the bread, said the blessing, broke it, and gave it to them, saying, 'This is my body, which will be given for you; do this in memory of me.' And likewise the cup after they had eaten, saying, 'This cup is the new covenant in my blood, which will be shed for you'" (Luke 22:19-20). In the context of the Jewish Passover sacrificial meal, Jesus gave his Church a sacrificial meal which would make him present to people of every age and touch their lives with the power of his love.

The Catholic Church calls this sacrificial meal the Eucharist, and we believe that Christ is as truly present in the sacrament of the Holy Eucharist as he was when he walked the streets of Jerusalem. We believe that the power of his loving death on the cross and of his Resurrection is made available to us through the Eucharist. In obedience to his wish, we do what Jesus did in memory of him.

Penance

When we apologize to another and say, "I'm sorry," we want to hear the words, "I forgive you." Jesus was God's Word of forgiveness to the sinners who came to him seeking pardon and peace. Sinners could look into his eyes and see love and compassion. They could hear from his lips words that made God's forgiveness certain, "Your sins are forgiven....Go in peace" (Luke 7:48,50).

Christ dealt with people in ways they could see, hear, and understand. Christ came to bring God's forgiveness to sinners. Therefore, it cannot be surprising that Christ gave to his followers a sign by which they could see, hear, and understand that he was always with them to forgive their sins. The Gospel of John reports that on Easter Sunday evening Jesus appeared to his apostles and said, "Receive the holy Spirit. Whose sins you forgive are forgiven them, and whose sins you retain are retained" (20:22-23).

The Catholic Church sees in this event Christ's gift of the sacrament of Penance. The apostles and their successors, the bishops, as well as the priests who are ministers with the bishops, are empowered by Christ to speak words of forgiveness in his name. In this sacrament, sinners of every age can receive the assurance of Christ's pardon and peace just as did those who heard the words, "Your sins are forgiven," from the lips of Christ himself.

Matrimony

The institution by Christ of Matrimony as a sacrament is not as obvious as that of the other sacraments. We cannot point to a single incident in Christ's life as the moment when marriage became a sacrament. The Church, reflecting on the Scriptures under the guidance of the Holy Spirit, only gradually came to the understanding of Matrimony as a sacrament given us by Christ.

From the very beginning, the Bible shows that marriage is not merely a human institution. It comes from God. "God created man in his image, in the divine image he created him; male and female he created them. God blessed them, saying: 'Be fertile and multiply'" (Genesis 1:27-28). Jesus clarified God's design for marriage in many ways. He was born into a family, thereby showing the holiness of family life (Luke 2). According to John's Gospel, he worked his first miracle at the wedding feast of Cana, thus putting his seal of approval on marriage (John 2:1-11). He taught that married love must be faithful (Matthew 5:27-28) and permanent (Mark 10:6-12). Saint Paul spoke of marriage as a sign, a sacrament, showing how Christ loves the Church: "'For this reason a man shall leave [his] father and [his] mother and be joined to his wife, and the two shall become one flesh.' This is a great mystery, but I speak in reference to Christ and the church" (Ephesians 5:31-32).

The Catholic Church, then, sees Matrimony as a sacrament which makes God's love visible and tangible here on earth. Husband and wife are the ministers of their sacrament of Matrimony (the priest or deacon is the official witness for the Church). Christ joins husband and wife together so that each can continue to minister his grace and be a living sign of God's love to the other and to their children. And just as Christ loved his apostles even with their weaknesses and frailties, so married couples are called to imitate Christ in making their love an everyday practical reality in spite of human failings. Real love is to be patient and kind. Like God's love, it must never fail (1 Corinthians 13).

When a husband and wife love each other as Christ does the Church, they welcome God into their everyday lives. God's love enters into such human activities as work and play, sexual relationships and raising children, health and sickness, sharing and forgiving, worship and prayer, life and death. Everything good that a husband and wife do for each other and for their children can bring them closer to God and to the happiness of heaven! God's love and grace are brought into our hearts and homes by the sacrament of Matrimony.

Holy Orders

The gospels show that early in his public ministry Jesus invited believers to follow him in a special way. These he called disciples (those who accept the teaching of a leader). From this group, he chose twelve men whom he named apostles (those who are sent). The apostles were ordinary men who left all to follow Christ. They traveled with him, witnessed his miracles, and received special instructions from him. At one point in his ministry, Christ sent the Twelve on mission to proclaim the kingdom of God and heal the sick. The Gospel of Matthew reports that Jesus said he would build his Church on Peter, first among the apostles (16:13-19). Christ gave them authority to speak in his name and to discipline those who refused to listen (Luke 10:16; Matthew 18:17). At the Last Supper, he asked the apostles to do what he had done (Luke 22:19). After his Resurrection, Jesus gave them the power to forgive sins (John 20:23) and sent them to preach and to baptize (Matthew 28:19).

The Catholic Church has seen Christ's directives to his apostles as evidence that Christ intended to send them and their successors as "sacramental signs" making him present to the world. They were to continue Christ's ministry of teaching, guiding, and sanctifying the human race for all time. The early Church valued a variety of ministries such as prophets, teachers, miracle workers, healers, helpers, administrators, interpreters (1 Corinthians 12:28), evangelists, pastors (Ephesians 4:11), deacons (Acts 6:1-6), presbyters (1 Timothy 5:17-22), and bishops (1 Timothy 2:1-7; Titus 1:5-9). The New Testament does not explain the interrelationships among these offices, and their functions probably varied in different locations.

But there is evidence from other sources that the offices of bishop, priest (presbyter), and deacon quickly began to take on the characteristics they now have in the Catholic Church. Ignatius of Antioch, who died in A.D. 108, wrote letters to local churches presided over by bishops, who were assisted by priests and deacons. He indicates that bishops and priests celebrated the Eucharist. Hippolytus of Rome, who died in A.D. 236, describes how the bishops ordained other bishops, priests, and deacons by the imposition of hands. This pattern of "ordination" is essential to the Catholic Church, which traces a line of succession from the apostles to the bishops of the present day.

In the gospels, the word *priest* is used to refer to the Jewish temple priesthood. But the Letter to the Hebrews calls Christ our high priest, and those who ministered in Christ's name soon came to be called priests. Those with the fullness of Christ's priesthood, who govern dioceses and are empowered to ordain other ministers are known as bishops. Assistants to the bishops who serve people in parish churches and who witness marriages and minister all the other sacraments except Holy Orders are usually called priests. Deacons are ordained helpers who preach, baptize, and witness marriages, but do not preside at other sacraments. These ministries have undergone many developments through the centuries, but the Catholic Church believes that in their essence they come from Christ himself. It is only reasonable to affirm that Christ, who came to make God's grace visible and tangible, should continue his ministry after his Resurrection. It is in keeping with the Incarnation that Christ should do this through ordained servants who would be "other Christs" in every time and place so that Christ could be with us always "until the end of the age" (Matthew 28:20).

Anointing of the Sick

Jesus came to bring God's mercy and healing to humanity, and the gospels state that Jesus worked many miracles of healing. Often he healed using signs that could be seen and felt. "At sunset, all who had people sick with various diseases brought them to him. He laid his hands on each of them and cured them" (Luke 4:40). He sent the twelve apostles to heal in his name, and they "anointed with oil many who were sick and cured them" (Mark 6:13).

The laying on of hands and anointing with oil were signs which mediated the power of God. After the Resurrection of Jesus, the

Church used prayer and anointing to bring Christ's healing to the sick: "Is anyone among you sick? He should summon the presbyters of the church, and they should pray over him and anoint [him] with oil in the name of the Lord, and the prayer of faith will save the sick person, and the Lord will raise him up. If he has committed any sins, he will be forgiven" (James 5:14-15). This passage is seen by the Catholic Church as Christ's design for the sacrament of Anointing of the Sick. It shows that such an anointing was given by the early Church, that the minister was a Church leader, and that Christ was present through the anointing to bring physical and spiritual healing.

It was obvious to the early Church, as it is to us today, that this mortal life must end in death. Therefore, while Anointing of the Sick often brings physical healing from illness and injury, there comes a time in the life of every human being when the anointing is the means by which Christ will raise us up to eternal life, which is the only complete healing. This sacrament, then, is the sign by which Christ continues his beautiful ministry of healing and of bestowing eternal life.

Christ Ministers Through the Sacraments

We have seen that the Catholic Church believes that Christ really "takes away the sin of the world" (John 1:29) and actually gives us "newness of life" (Romans 6:4), which is a share in the life of God. We call this new life "sanctifying grace." Just as Christ gave such life to the people of his own time, so he continues to minister this life to us through the sacraments.

Some Christians believe that Christ merely "covers over" our sins and that Christ's holiness is merely "imputed" to us (extrinsic justification). They do not accept the reality of sanctifying grace, and therefore do not understand the sacraments as we do, as signs by which Christ takes away sin and bestows grace. They see Baptism or the Eucharist as symbols which remind us of Christ, but not as signs through which Christ actually is present to us to give us life and grace.

When we Catholics see how Christ worked real changes in people like the apostles, Mary Magdalene, and the repentant thief on the cross, we do not find it difficult to believe that he still works such changes today. When Catholics see that God was actually

73

born into the world and placed in a manger, we are not surprised to find God coming to us in water, bread, and wine. We believe that God takes us as we really are—people who need physical signs because we are ourselves body as well as spirit. We know that just as God came to the world in a visible, tangible way in the birth of Christ, so Christ comes to us in visible, tangible ways in the sacraments.

We who are Catholic are privileged to be members of a family which has always treasured the sacraments. Through them, Christ hugs and heals, unites and forgives, forever joining us to God in a wonderful embrace of the human and divine.

Questions for Discussion and Reflection

What are some "signs of love," such as keepsakes and gifts from family and friends, which you value in a special way? How do they make loved ones present to you? In what ways are the sacraments like these signs? In what ways do the sacraments surpass such signs?

Can you name the seven sacraments from memory? How many sacraments have you received? Did you think of them as meetings with Christ? Were you aware that Christ was doing the same things for you that he did for his own contemporaries? If we have not been as aware of these realities in the past, is it too late for us to benefit from such an awareness now, even for sacraments which cannot be repeated?

Activities

Take out any keepsakes, photographs, and souvenirs associated with sacraments you have received, such as Baptism, first Holy Communion, Confirmation, or Marriage. Spend some time examining these remembrances. Recall the moment you received the sacraments associated with them. Think of how these sacraments have intertwined your life with the life of Jesus Christ. Thank Jesus for the sacraments, signs of his love for you.

CHAPTER SEVEN
The Eucharist

Friends like to be together. In recalling special times of togetherness, we likely think of meals shared with friends and family—Thanksgiving dinners, birthday parties, family picnics.

Jesus loved to be with people, and he enjoyed sharing meals with them. It is not surprising, then, that when Jesus sought a way to be close to us, he chose a meal. On the night before he died, he celebrated the Jewish Passover meal with his apostles. This meal recalled God's deliverance of the Israelites from slavery in Egypt and anticipated the salvation the Israelites hoped would be given them through the long-expected Messiah. Jesus was, of course, that Messiah, the Savior, and God's salvation was about to be brought to all humanity by Christ's loving death on the cross.

The Eucharist: Meal and Real Presence

At the meal, Jesus "took bread, said the blessing, broke it, and giving it to his disciples said, 'Take and eat; this is my body.' Then he took a cup, gave thanks, and gave it to them, saying, 'Drink from it, all of you, for this is my blood of the covenant, which will be shed on behalf of many for the forgiveness of sins'" (Matthew 26:26-28).

The Catholic Church has always believed that when Jesus said these words, he meant exactly what he said. For Jews of Jesus' time, *body* meant the person, and *blood* was the source of life identifiable with the person. So Jesus was saying over the bread and wine, "This is my very self." He used material things, bread and wine, to make himself really present to believers of every age. This seems almost too good to be true, and from the very beginning until the present day, some have not been able to accept Jesus at his word.

The Gospel of John records that Jesus in an instruction at Capernaum had said: "I am the living bread that came down from heaven; whoever eats this bread will live forever; and the bread that I will give is my flesh for the life of the world" (6:51). Many of his listeners objected to this statement, so Jesus declared: "Amen, amen, I say to you, unless you eat the flesh of the Son of Man and drink his blood, you do not have life within you. Whoever eats my flesh and drinks my blood has eternal life, and I will raise him on the last day. For my flesh is true food, and my blood is true drink. Whoever eats my flesh and drinks my blood remains in me and I in him" (6:53-56).

These words shocked his followers. "This saying is hard"; they asked, "Who can accept it?" (6:60) Many "returned to their former way of life and no longer accompanied him" (6:66). Jesus did not run after them and shout, "Don't go away. You misunderstood. I didn't mean that the bread *is* my body, but only that it *represents* my body." Instead, he asked his apostles, "Do you also want to leave?" Peter answered, "Master, to whom shall we go? You have the words of eternal life. We have come to believe and are convinced that you are the Holy One of God" (6:67-69).

Jesus, when confronted with the difficulty of what he was saying, did not "water down" his statements in the least. They were indeed hard to accept and impossible to understand. But Peter did not claim to understand them. He simply accepted them on the authority of Jesus, who had "the words of eternal life."

Saint Paul also trusted in the authority of Jesus. He believed that Jesus meant what he said in the words, "This is my body." After criticizing the Corinthians for irreverence in the way they received the Eucharist, he stated bluntly, "Whoever eats the bread or drinks the cup of the Lord unworthily will have to answer for the body and blood of the Lord" (1 Corinthians 11:27).

We Catholics have always put our faith in the authority of Jesus and have believed in the Real Presence of Jesus under the appearances of bread and wine. We believe because the Real Presence is no more incredible than the Incarnation itself. If God would become human to make divinity present to us, why would Christ not change bread and wine into his divinity and humanity? Why would he, who enjoyed being close to friends at meals, not choose a meal to grant to his friends the gift of the closest possible intimacy? Catholic belief in the Real Presence fits into our pattern of accepting the deep-down goodness of God's creation, and of knowing that God actually uses material things to give us divine love and grace. Bread and wine, then, are changed by Christ into himself in a miracle of love we Catholics call the "Blessed Sacrament."

Catholic Doctrine and Christ's Real Presence

The fact that Christ's words, "This is my body; this is my blood," caused bread and wine to become himself was a miracle. Christ made this miracle available to people of all time when he said to his apostles, and to their successors, "Do this in memory of me" (Luke 22:19). The Catholic Church believes that when a priest speaks the words of Jesus, the "words of consecration," over the bread and wine, the miracle of the Last Supper is made present to us today. The bread and wine become Jesus Christ.

The traditional Catholic term for this miracle has been *transubstantiation*. It means that the "substance" of the bread and wine becomes the "substance" of Christ's body and blood, while the appearances of bread and wine remain. When we receive Holy Communion, then, we truly receive the body and blood, soul and divinity, of the Lord Jesus Christ, under the appearance of bread and wine. This terminology is rather technical, but it was used by the Council of Trent because it expresses clearly that the bread and wine become Christ.

The "separate consecration" of the bread and wine ("This is my body; this is my blood") serves as a reminder that Christ's blood was separated from his body when he died on the cross. When the Eucharist is celebrated today, however, Christ's blood is not separated from his body. The Christ who becomes present at the words of consecration is the risen, glorified Christ. He is fully present under the appearances of bread or wine, and we receive Christ when we take communion under the form of bread or wine.

Not all Christians believe in the Eucharist as Catholics do. Some believe that Christ is present along with the bread and wine; they assert that in taking communion they are receiving bread and wine, *in which* Jesus is present. Some maintain that Christ is present, not as a result of the power of Christ but as a result of their personal belief. Some say that Christ is present only as a result of the faith of the community; they do not believe that Christ remains present after the worship service. Some deny that Christ is really present; they contend that they are receiving bread and wine which symbolize the spirit and teachings of Jesus, and that in doing so they are expressing their attachment to his person and words. There are many variations on these themes, and Catholics should carefully distinguish the official teaching of the Catholic Church on the Eucharist from other opinions.

The Special Nature of Christ's Eucharistic Presence

Many people, after receiving Holy Communion or while making a visit to Christ in the sacrament of the Eucharist, have been blessed with a powerful sense of Christ's Real Presence. We Catholics believe, of course, that once the words of Christ are said over the bread and wine, they become Christ and remain Christ as long as the appearances of bread and wine remain. We keep the Eucharist, the "Blessed Sacrament," in the church in a tabernacle (from a Latin word meaning "tent"), because we believe that Christ remains truly present.

We may wonder, however, about the nature of this presence. After all, Christ is God, and God is everywhere. What is so special about the fact that Christ is present in the Eucharist?

First, there is a physical presence through the signs of bread and wine that is special. God was everywhere before the Incarnation, but the physical presence of the human body of Christ allowed people to see, hear, and touch God. Christ is everywhere in his glorified state now, but the physical presence of the Eucharist allows us to look upon Christ and touch Christ (under the appearances of bread and wine).

Second, to say that God is everywhere is to say that God is infinite, without limits. We are human, however; we are finite, limited. We do not relate easily to the infinite. That is one of the reasons why God took on a human body and became one of us. The Incarnation allowed people to "locate" God, to see and touch God when they saw and touched Jesus Christ. Similarly, the Eucharist locates the presence of Jesus. Christ can once again be seen and touched, and even more, received into our own being. Receiving Jesus Christ in Holy Communion allows us to remain in him and him in us (John 6:56). Visiting Christ as he is truly present in the Eucharist gets us out of the generality of "everywhere" into a specific time and place, where we can be with the Lord, as were Andrew and another disciple who followed Jesus and stayed with him for a day's visit (John 1:35-40).

Third, the fact that Christ is present under the appearances of bread and wine that are to be taken as food reminds us that Christ wants more than a casual, distant relationship with us. He could have chosen many other ways to make his presence available to us. But the Eucharist shows us that Christ wants to be close to us, that he invites us into a friendship of intimacy and love (John 15:15; 17:20-26). There are many ways of "being together." A mother and her infant, for example, might be together in the same house. They are much closer together, however, when she holds her child in her arms. The Eucharist invites us to the closest possible intimacy with Jesus Christ, a union that is both spiritual and physical.

Fourth, when Christ gave us the Eucharist, he said that his body would be "given" for us (Luke 22:19) and that his blood would be "shed" (Matthew 26:28) for us. The Eucharist, therefore, is a constant reminder that the Christ present before us is the one who gave his life for us, his friends (John 15:13). The Eucharist assures us that no love could be greater than Christ's love for us. The Eucharist invites us to imitate the generous love of Christ by giving of ourselves for the sake of others.

Finally, the Eucharist we worship at Mass or in quiet prayer is always the Jesus who is being worshiped all over the world by believers of our Catholic family. This tabernacle, this place where Christ is sacramentally present, can and should remind us of tabernacles in every land where Christ is being honored by our brothers and sisters. The Eucharist is a sign that we are never alone because we are members of the Body of Christ.

The Eucharist:
Christ's Sacrifice Made Present for Us

We have spoken of the Eucharist as the presence of Jesus made available to us when bread and wine are transformed into Christ. But the word *eucharist* also refers to what we celebrate in response to Christ's command, "Do this in memory of me." What we celebrate is referred to as the "eucharistic sacrifice," the "sacrifice of the Mass," the "eucharistic liturgy." This is, of course, the sacramental action which makes Christ truly present; the sacrifice of the Mass and the Real Presence of Christ are two aspects of the sacrament of the Eucharist.

In many ways, the liturgy (from a Greek word meaning "public ritual" or "work") of the Mass is similar to the Last Supper. At the Last Supper, Jesus and the apostles sang hymns, read sacred Scripture, prayed, and shared a sacrificial meal. The first part of the Mass (Liturgy of the Word) is made up of hymns, prayers, and readings from sacred Scripture. At the Last Supper, Jesus offered himself in a loving sacrifice "for the forgiveness of sins" (Matthew 26:28), changed bread and wine into his body and blood, which he gave to his apostles in the first eucharistic "Communion." In the second part of the Mass (Liturgy of the Eucharist), the priest offers a eucharistic prayer in which he repeats Jesus' words of consecration over the bread and wine, and the faithful receive Christ in Communion as did the apostles.

The Catholic Church teaches that the eucharistic liturgy is a sacrifice. Jesus gave his life on the cross, the greatest sacrifice imaginable. The Last Supper anticipated his sacrificial death, and each celebration of the Eucharist recalls the sacrificial death of Jesus. "At the Last Supper, on the night when He was betrayed, our Savior instituted the Eucharistic Sacrifice of His Body and Blood. He did this in order to perpetuate the sacrifice of the Cross throughout the centuries until He should come again" (SVC, *The Constitution on the Sacred Liturgy,* 47). This does not mean that Christ dies again (Hebrews 7:27). The Mass does not *repeat* the death of Christ, but makes it *present* to us. "The cup of blessing that we bless, is it not a participation in the blood of Christ? The bread that we break, is it not a participation in the body of Christ?" (1 Corinthians 10:16)

A Sacrifice Making Present What Was Past

The Eucharist is a sacrament, a sign, that miraculously rolls away the centuries and allows us to participate in the Last Supper, stand at the cross of Christ, and experience the glory of the risen Lord. In Saint Paul's words, "As often as you eat this bread and drink the cup, you proclaim the death of the Lord until he comes" (1 Corinthians 11:26), we note the Last Supper ("eat...drink"), the cross ("death of the Lord"), and the glory ("until he comes"). We are not imagining things, therefore, if we at times participate in the Mass by picturing ourselves at the Last Supper, at the cross on Calvary, or at the empty tomb.

On some occasions, we may relate the various parts of the Mass to the Last Supper. As we enter the church where Mass is to be celebrated, we can see ourselves gathering with Jesus and the apostles in the upper room, for Christ "is present when the Church prays and sings" (SVC, *Liturgy*, 7). As Scripture readings are proclaimed, we can picture Christ as reader, for Christ is present "in His word, since it is He Himself who speaks when the holy Scriptures are read in the church" (SVC, *Liturgy*, 7). When the priest says the words of consecration, we should hear Christ saying those words, and when we take Holy Communion, we may receive the Lord, as did the apostles, from the hands of the Lord. This is the reality, for Christ "is present in the sacrifice of the Mass, not only in the person of His minister, 'the same one now offering, through the ministry of priests, who formerly offered himself on the cross,' but especially under the Eucharistic species" (SVC, *Liturgy*, 7).

On other occasions when we celebrate Mass, we may wish to picture ourselves at Calvary. We gather at the foot of the cross with Mary and the faithful women, with the beloved disciple, and with other believers. The Penitential Rite is a special time to realize that our sins helped cause Christ's agony, and we express our sorrow. We may think of the Scripture readings as Jesus' words to us from the cross. We should relate the separate consecration of bread and wine to the fact that Christ gave his body and shed his blood for us. We receive the risen Christ in Holy Communion with the awareness that Mary once had to receive the broken body of Christ from the cross into her arms. We thank Christ for loving us even to death on the cross.

On still other occasions, especially during the Easter season, we may relate the Mass to the Resurrection of Christ. We can gather with the women at the empty tomb, or with the apostles in the upper room, knowing that we will see in the Eucharist the one they saw on that first Easter Sunday. Like the two disciples on the way to Emmaus, we can listen as Christ explains the Scriptures. We recognize him as they did when "he took bread, said the blessing, broke it, and give it to them" (Luke 24:13-35). As we receive Christ in Holy Communion, we profess our faith in the risen Lord in the words of Thomas the Apostle, "My Lord and my God!" (John 20:28)

A Sacrifice Anticipating the Future

The Mass not only makes present the past, it anticipates the future. When Saint Paul said that through the Eucharist we proclaim the death of the Lord "until he comes," he was referring primarily to Christ's Second Coming at the end of time. But we are not distorting the meaning of his words if we also apply them to Christ's coming at the moment of our death.

The Eucharist is a pledge that we will live forever. We receive in Holy Communion our risen Lord, who has promised that we too shall rise. Death could not conquer Christ, and through our union with Christ in the Blessed Sacrament we are assured that death will not conquer us. "Whoever eats my flesh and drinks my blood has eternal life, and I will raise him on the last day....Whoever eats this bread will live forever" (John 6:54,58). We who celebrate the Eucharist with faith and receive the risen Lord in Holy Communion are promised that Christ, "who lives and reigns forever and ever" will one day take us by the hand and lead us through death to the fullness of eternal life.

"In the earthly liturgy, by way of foretaste, we share in that heavenly liturgy which is celebrated in the holy city of Jerusalem toward which we journey as pilgrims, and in which Christ is sitting at the right hand of God....we eagerly await the Savior, our Lord Jesus Christ, until He, our life, shall appear and we too will appear with Him in glory (cf. Philippians 3:20; Colossians 3:4)" (SVC, *Liturgy*, 8).

Body of Christ and Communion of Saints

The Eucharist, as sacrifice and Communion, is a sacrament that unites those who participate in the Mass. Christ is present in the gathering of the faithful to make them one. "For where two or three are gathered together in my name, there am I in the midst of them"

(Matthew 18:20). Those who receive Holy Communion are joined as one, because they receive the same Christ. "Because the loaf of bread is one, we, though many, are one body, for we all partake of the one loaf" (1 Corinthians 10:17).

And if we are united to Christ, we are united also to members of his Body throughout the world and to the saints in heaven who see Christ face to face. At every Mass, "we are surrounded by so great a cloud of witnesses" (Hebrews 12:1), a fact recognized in the eucharistic prayers. We are never closer to heaven than when we celebrate the Mass and receive into our hearts the Lord before whom "every knee should bend, of those in heaven and on earth" (Philippians 2:10). At Mass, "we sing a hymn to the Lord's glory with all the warriors of the heavenly army; venerating the memory of the saints, we hope for some part and fellowship with them" (SVC, *Liturgy*, 8).

The communion of saints includes, of course, our loved ones who have died. At Mass, we are close to our friends and family in heaven; they pray with us and for us. Parents should remind their children that they can pray to "Grandma" at Mass, and that she will be watching over them. This awareness can help make the Mass special to children, and to all of us.

Our Part in the Sacrifice

The incredible realities of the Eucharist are brought to us in signs, in rituals based on what Jesus did at the Last Supper and developed through nearly twenty centuries of worship. This is a great blessing, for the ritual ceremonies of the Mass provide a pattern of worship into which we can fit our own circumstances, our desire to adore, thank, seek forgiveness, and ask for what we need. We do not have to "reinvent the wheel" every Sunday. In a world where everything seems to be changing and where so many demands come at us from so many directions, we need a solid, unchanging foundation for our lives. There is no more solid foundation than the Eucharist, for "Jesus Christ is the same yesterday, today, and forever" (Hebrews 13:8).

In the Mass, we have a comfortable, time-tested pattern for worship. However, we must not allow the ritual of the Mass to become routine. We must personalize the ritual by our own active participation and involvement.

We do this by taking the time to study the Mass and pray about our participation in the Mass. We must never forget that our presence at the Mass is important to Jesus Christ. The Mass is the one thing Christ asked us to do in memory of him (Luke 22:19), a fact we should recall when we don't "feel like going to Mass"!

Without each member of the Body of Christ, the eucharistic celebration is not all it could be. When we attend Mass, we are not simply appearing at an event with many other individuals who happen to be there, as is the case when we go to a movie or sporting event. Rather, we are attending a family reunion, for the Mass is the gathering of the members of Christ's Body.

Further, we bring a gift to Mass which no one else can offer. We bring ourselves, the circumstances of our lives, our ups and our downs, what we've done, and what we hope to accomplish with God's help. We bring our own prayers, our greeting to others, our offering for the Lord. We may not realize how important our presence is to Christ, but if we consider how much Christ appreciated the loving repentance of a sinful woman (Luke 7:36-50), the humble prayer of a mother (Matthew 15:21-28), the profession of faith by Peter (Matthew 16:13-19), a widow's gift of two copper coins (Mark 12:41-44), and an anointing with perfumed oil (Matthew 26:6-13), we will begin to see how much Christ wants and appreciates what we have to offer.

When we celebrate the sacrifice of the Mass and receive the Lord in Holy Communion, we are helped to be the Body of Christ in the world today. As Christ gave of himself, even to the extent of washing his apostles' feet on the night before he died, so ought we to give of ourselves in loving service (John 13:1-20). As Christ loved us even to death on the cross, so ought we to love one another (John 15:12-13). When the Mass is ended, we are to go in peace to love and serve the Lord and one another.

"The Church, therefore, earnestly desires that Christ's faithful, when present at this mystery of faith, should not be there as strangers or silent spectators. On the contrary, through a proper appreciation of the rites and prayers they should participate knowingly, devoutly, and actively. They should be instructed by God's word and be refreshed at the table of the Lord's body; they should give thanks to God; by offering the Immaculate Victim, not only through the hands of the priest, but also with him, they should learn to offer themselves too. Through Christ the Mediator, they should be drawn day by day into ever closer union with God and with each other, so that finally God may be all in all" (SVC, *Liturgy*, 48).

"My Lord and My God!"

The apostle Thomas, according to the Gospel of John, was not with the other apostles when they saw the risen Lord on Easter Sunday evening. He doubted until Christ appeared to him, invited him to touch the wounds of crucifixion, and encouraged him with the words, "Do not be unbelieving, but believe." Thomas then professed his faith in Jesus: "My Lord and my God!" (John 20: 27-28).

Something like that happens at every Mass. Jesus does not appear in bodily form, but he comes among us in the gathering of the community, the person of his minister, the power of his Word, and the sacrament of the Eucharist. These signs are set into many others, the sights, sounds, scents, touches, and tastes that invite us to perceive the Lord with our whole being. The sights of altar, candles, vestments, stained glass, sacred images, flowers; the sounds of Word, song, music, prayer; the scents of flowers and incense; the touch of a neighbor's hand and of Christ's body in ours; the tastes of what had been bread and wine but are now Christ's body and blood. All these signs summon us toward the Lord and to the altar call that is Holy Communion, so that like Thomas we may say, "My Lord and my God!" We do not see Jesus as Thomas did, but we see him with eyes of faith in the signs of the Eucharist, and we are blessed because we believe.

It is an awesome privilege for us to be part of a Catholic family which has always believed in the Real Presence and in the sacrifice of the Mass. It is an even more awesome privilege to share in that sacrifice and to receive our Lord and God in Holy Communion.

Questions for Discussion and Reflection

What do you remember about your first Holy Communion? Can you recall how you felt about receiving Jesus into your heart? About how many times have you received Communion in your lifetime? Have you considered that you are receiving the same Christ whom you will meet at the moment of death?

Have you ever wished that you could have been present at the Last Supper, or at Calvary, or at the Resurrection of Jesus? Are you excited by the fact that you are really present at these saving events when you attend Mass?

Have you ever thought of Communion as an "altar call," where we accept Christ as our Lord and Savior, as our Lord and God?

Activities

Make a visit to Christ in the Blessed Sacrament. Spend a few minutes coming to the realization that Christ is really present in the tabernacle. Talk to Jesus about anything you wish. Ask him to help you be more aware of his presence at every Mass and in the Blessed Sacrament.

As suggested earlier in this chapter, when you attend Mass, picture yourself at the Last Supper or Calvary or at Easter Sunday with Jesus. Or you can picture yourself at all three events: be with Jesus at the Last Supper from the first part of the Mass until the words of consecration; then stand under the cross with Mary through the Lord's prayer; finally, enjoy the presence of the risen Lord until the end of Mass.

CHAPTER EIGHT
The Sacrament
of Penance

S ome years ago I participated with parents and teachers in a program to prepare a group of second graders for their first celebration of the sacrament of Penance. The children were taught that Jesus loved them and wanted them to love others, that our sins hurt others and offend Jesus, that Jesus comes in the sacrament of Penance to listen to our apologies and to tell us that he forgives our sins. After the celebration of the sacrament, a little boy came running up to me with the words, "That was fun, Father! When can we do it again?"

I'd never really thought of the sacrament of Penance as "fun," but that little boy captured something of the enthusiasm we Catholics ought to have for a sacrament which is one of Christ's greatest gifts, but which is often not properly understood. When we repent of our sins, tell God that we are sorry, and ask for forgiveness, the sacrament of Penance allows us to hear Jesus Christ accept our apology.

Offenses and Apologies

We have all had the experience of offending another through our own fault. In a moment of anger, for example, we spoke harsh words to a friend. Then, realizing that we had done wrong, we felt guilt and regret. We went to the friend and apologized: "I am sorry. Please forgive me." We waited anxiously for a response, and were relieved and happy to hear the words, "I forgive you."

If there had been no response to our apology, we would not have known where we stood. Silence might have indicated that the friend had refused to accept the apology. It might have indicated that our friend simply did not know how to respond. We might have wondered if we should apologize again or simply walk away. If apologies are not accepted in some obvious way, uncertainties and doubts result.

Apologies Accepted

God created the world "very good" and invited human beings, who were made in the "divine image," to govern it according to God's plan. But the first human beings rejected God's invitation. They chose to do evil rather than good, and sin entered the world. With sin came guilt and regret, as those first human beings realized that they had done something terribly wrong in disobeying God.

Their sin has been repeated by countless generations of human beings. Countless generations have felt guilt and remorse and have tried to "apologize" to God. They expressed sorrow for their sins and sought God's forgiveness (Psalm 51).

The people of the Old Testament believed that God forgave repentant sinners, but their understanding of God's revelation was imperfect. The stories they told about Abraham and Moses, for example, suggested that God had to be persuaded to show mercy and forgiveness (Genesis 18:16-33; Exodus 32:1-14). Their story of David and Bathsheba indicated a belief that God would actually cause the death of an innocent child to punish parents for their sins (2 Samuel 12:13-25). They seemed to think that God was saying, "I forgive you, but...."

The pagan world in Old Testament times was largely ignorant of God's mercy. Human beings were held captive by sin and for the most part did not even seek God's forgiveness (Romans 1-3).

God's response to the uncertainties of the Jews and to the ignorance of pagans was the Incarnation. When the Word became flesh in Jesus Christ, people could look into the eyes of God and see compassion and love (Luke 19:1-10). They could hear God speak words of forgiveness (Luke 7:36-50). Before the Incarnation, people wondered if God would forgive their sins. In the presence of Jesus, people could be certain of God's pardon and peace. He showed them that when they sincerely said the words, "I am sorry; please forgive me," God's response was, "I forgive you."

Signs of Mercy and Forgiveness

The New Testament leaves no room for doubt in its presentation of Jesus' teaching and attitudes about forgiveness. Jesus created some of his most vivid parables to show that God is eager to forgive us and rejoices when we seek pardon for our sins. The three parables of forgiveness in Luke 15, for example, present God as someone who seeks out what is lost and then rejoices over what is found. A shepherd searches for a lost sheep, a woman looks for a lost coin, a father longs for a lost son. The shepherd, the woman, and the father rediscover that which was lost, and they celebrate by having a party. Clearly, God does not have to be persuaded to forgive us, nor does God grant pardon in a grim and grudging way.

What Jesus taught in words, he demonstrated by his actions. He showed compassion to sinners, who came seeking forgiveness, and spoke the words they wanted to hear: "Your sins are forgiven....Go in peace" (Luke 7:48,50). He celebrated at dinner parties when sinners like Matthew and Zacchaeus were reconciled with God (Matthew 9:9-13; Luke 19:1-10). At his crucifixion, he prayed for those who persecuted him: "Father, forgive them, they know not what they do" (Luke 23:34). When one of the criminals nailed beside him pleaded, "Jesus, remember me when you come into your kingdom," Jesus assured him of pardon: "Amen, I say to you, today you will be with me in Paradise" (Luke 23:42-43).

Those who expressed their sorrow for sin were given unmistakable signs that they were forgiven. By his words and actions, Jesus assured them of God's eagerness to forgive them and of God's joy at their return to God's presence.

The Sacrament of Penance

Jesus knew that repentant sinners of every age would need to hear him say, "I forgive you." According to the Gospel of John, on Easter Sunday evening Jesus instituted a sacrament to make this possible. "On the evening of that first day of the week, when the doors were locked, where the disciples were, for fear of the Jews, Jesus came and stood in their midst and said to them, 'Peace be with you.' When he had said this, he showed them his hands and his side. The disciples rejoiced when they saw the Lord. [Jesus] said to them again, 'Peace be with you. As the Father has sent me, so I send you.' And when he had said this, he breathed on them and said to them, 'Receive the holy Spirit. Whose sins you forgive are forgiven them, and whose sins you retain are retained'" (John 20:19-23).

The apostles must have been amazed when Jesus said these words. We can imagine them responding, "Lord, we need *your* forgiveness. We ran away when you were arrested. We are sorry. Please forgive *us*." And Jesus might have answered: "Yes, I know you are sorry, and I forgive you. But down through the ages there will be many others who will fail as you have failed. They, too, will regret their sins and will want to be assured of my forgiveness. I want to speak words of pardon and peace through you and through those who will follow in your footsteps. When you forgive others, I forgive them."

Catholics believe that Christ gave his Church the sacrament of Penance (also called Confession or the sacrament of Reconciliation) when he said, "Receive the holy Spirit. Whose sins you forgive are forgiven them, and whose sins you retain are retained." The sacramental signs were, and are, confession of sins to a minister of the Church and an expression of God's forgiveness to the repentant sinner.

In the early days of the Church, those who sinned after Baptism were reconciled to the Church through the bishop. The sacrament of Penance was applied primarily to serious sins such as adultery, apostasy, and murder. Usually, sinners went through a long period of public penance and were reconciled to the Church at Easter. In the sixth century, through the influence of Irish monks, Penance became available for less serious sins, and private confession of sins replaced the rigorous discipline of earlier times.

In the twelfth century, the theology of Penance took on dimensions that shaped usage of the sacrament to our own day. Theologians explained that Penance included contrition (sorrow and conversion), confession of sins to a priest, satisfaction (doing penance for one's sins and making up for any harm done by those sins), and absolution (declaration of forgiveness) by a priest.

These four elements were affirmed by the Council of Trent in 1551 after the sacraments were questioned by Protestants. By the twentieth century, it was common for Catholics to go to confession quite frequently, usually following a set pattern.

Vatican II called for a revision of Penance in order to express more clearly its nature and effects. (See SVC, *Liturgy*, 72.) A new Rite of Reconciliation was established in 1974. It expanded the use of Scripture, emphasized the role of the priest as a healer in Christ's name, pointed out the importance of the Church in reconciling us with God, and offered various options for the reception of the sacrament.

Why a Sacrament of Forgiveness?

In recent years, many Catholics have been using the sacrament of Penance rarely, if at all. Some of them even echo an old objection: "Why confess to a priest? Why not confess sins directly to Christ?"

The answer is, of course, that we are human. We need signs. When we have offended another, we need to express our sorrow. Hard as it may be, we need to find words to admit our guilt and seek forgiveness. And after we have apologized, we need to hear someone say, "I forgive you."

This is true when we seek God's forgiveness. We need to get our sins out in the open by acknowledging them. We do this by confessing our sins to the Church's minister, who is a sign that Christ is present. We need to hear Christ say, "Your sins are forgiven." We hear these words when Christ speaks through the priest.

Interestingly, many prominent Protestant leaders are now saying that it is not enough just to "confess our sins to God." They point out the necessity of confessing our sins to another human being. Even when they do not speak of such "confessing" as a sacrament, they explain that it offers many spiritual benefits.

Perhaps the main reason for this has been the success and growth of Twelve Step programs like Alcoholics Anonymous. Millions of people have been helped through such programs, and the steps closely resemble the process of making a good confession. We admit our need for God. We examine our lives for any wrongdoing. We admit our sins, honestly and clearly, to God, to ourselves, and to another person. We look to God to help us overcome our weaknesses. We make amends to those we have wronged.

Doctor Norman Vincent Peale, in an article in *Guideposts* magazine (April 1989), praises the Twelve Step program as a means of spiritual growth. In particular, he states that the requirement to admit our faults to another person is of great importance because it brings any guilty secrets into the open where they can be dealt with.

Reverend Robert Schuller, in his book *The Be-Happy Attitudes* (page 127), writes that if we have a secret that we have never shared with any other human being about something we have done or have thought about doing which is illegal or immoral, we are not free of negative emotions. Such negative emotions can keep us from putting our faith in God.

Richard Foster, a well-known Quaker minister, teacher and author, has an entire chapter on confession in his book *The Celebration of Discipline: The Path to Spiritual Growth.* After describing patterns for confession very much like those used in the Catholic Church, he explains the many blessings that flow from confession. He affirms that God is calling all Christians to confess their sins and to experience the forgiving graces of Christ.

This helps us understand why the Catholic Church believes that Christ wants us to confess our sins to a priest and hear words of forgiveness from the priest. Confession and absolution fit into the very human pattern of apologizing for our failings and being granted forgiveness when we ask pardon.

Ordinary human experience also shows the value of being able to talk to another about our guilt. Consider the situation where a friend says, "Something is bothering me. I feel very bad about it and just don't know what to do." Our first response would most likely be, "Would you like to talk about it?" Healing begins when we are able to get sin and guilt outside ourselves where it can be dealt with.

Many psychologists are now saying that when we keep guilt and other negative feelings inside, they cause stress which is harmful to our emotional and physical health. The same psychologists point out that talking about our guilt with another person has a cleansing effect and helps us gain new insights to face the future. Our sins and our failings seem less overwhelming when we "get them out of our system." We can face them honestly and see that, while we may have done something bad, we can deal with it.

These positive effects of confession, now being recognized by psychologists, were known two thousand years ago by Jesus Christ, who understands human nature better than anyone else! So he chose confession and absolution as signs which make him really present to hear our sins and tell us that we are forgiven. And this is, of course, the greatest benefit of the sacrament of Penance.

Admitting guilt is not easy, but it is good for us. It brings physical, emotional, and spiritual healing. "Therefore, confess your sins to one another and pray for one another, that you may be healed" (James 5:16).

The Value of the Sacrament of Penance

The Catholic Church has always treasured the sacrament of Penance, but today we may need to regain our appreciation of this sacrament. The sacrament of Penance is a great gift from Jesus. We will make the best use of it when we realize its tremendous value and the many benefits it conveys.

First, the sacrament of Penance fits into the Catholic understanding of the sacramental principle. God deals with us as human beings, who are both body and soul. We need to express sorrow and to receive assurance that we are forgiven in physical, external ways. God became human in Jesus Christ in order to allow people to express their sorrow to another human being and to receive signs of forgiveness from another human being. Christ continues the Incarnation through his Church, allowing people to confess their sins to and receive certainty of forgiveness from other human beings who are signs of his presence. In fact, it would be surprising if Jesus, who came to take away the sins of the world, had *not* granted the Church a way to provide assurance of forgiveness to repentant sinners!

Second, the sacrament of Penance helps us confront the problem of serious sin. Out of weakness or malice, people may do shameful things, then think, "If others knew me as I really am, they would not accept me." Such people put themselves at the bottom of the human race. But when a sinner confesses, then is accepted and assured of God's pardon, that sinner begins to realize: "Yes, I have done evil things, but I am not evil. If the confessor and God accept me, then I can accept myself as a good and lovable person who has done evil, but now wishes to turn away from sin."

Third, the sacrament of Penance helps us deal with less serious failings. We can drift along in life, spiritually lazy, failing to recognize in ourselves the "little" sins like selfishness, gossip, and impatience. People who use the sacrament of Penance faithfully are encouraged thereby to examine their conscience, take stock of their failings, and look to God for the forgiveness and help only God can give.

Fourth, the sacrament of Penance helps us realize that sin is never trivial. Sin is always an offense against God. Sin crucified our Savior. Confession reminds us that sin must never be taken lightly. We know this, at least in theory, but we must have a way of putting theory into practice. Each time we celebrate the sacrament of Penance, we leave the realm of theory. We experience in a practical way the holiness of God and our own need for God's forgiveness and grace.

Fifth, the sacrament of Penance illustrates the fact that sin is not just a "personal matter" between myself and God. Since the Church is the Body of Christ, every sin against Christ harms the Church in some way, and reconciliation with Christ requires reconciliation with the Church. Confession allows this because the priest is a representative of the Church and because we receive the sacrament as members of the Church.

Celebrating the Sacrament of Penance

Most Catholic parishes have scheduled times for the sacrament of Penance when a priest is available at the church to hear confessions. Many parishes have communal Penance services scheduled at special times of the year, usually during Lent and Advent. People assemble for prayers, hymns, Scripture readings, examination of conscience, and an Act of Sorrow, then individual confessions and absolution. Catholics may also make an appointment with any priest to receive the sacrament of Penance.

We should receive the sacrament of Penance by praying for the grace to see ourselves as Christ does, by examining our conscience, being truly sorry for our failings, confessing our sins, receiving absolution, fulfilling the penance we are given, and then doing our best to make up for any harm done against others and to avoid the sins we have confessed. Whether we celebrate this sacrament privately or in Penance services, *Jesus* is always there, taking away sin and guilt and assuring us that we are forgiven.

Jesus is also present in the sacrament of Penance to teach us how to forgive. Since he is so ready to forgive us, we ought to do our best to forgive others. When others apologize, we should imitate Christ in saying, "I forgive you." Even when others offend us and do not ask for pardon, we should turn to Christ for the grace and strength to put away hatred and revenge. We should pray for those who harm us as he prayed for those who crucified him. This is very difficult, of course, but with the grace of God it is possible. And that is what we pray for each time we say, "Forgive us our trespasses as we forgive those who trespass against us."

The Priest, a Sign of Christ's Forgiving Presence

The Catholic Church believes that the proper ministers of the sacrament of Penance are the successors of the apostles, the bishops, as well as their ordained priest-helpers. The role of the priest in this sacrament is to be a sign of Christ's forgiving presence.

This may be hard to realize. Some people of Jesus' time objected when he told individuals that their sins were forgiven. "Who but God alone can forgive sins?" (Mark 2:7) They did not understand that Jesus *was* God. Today, some people say that we should confess our sins to Christ alone, not to a priest. They do not realize the full meaning of sacrament, for the priest is a sacramental sign making Christ present. When we confess our sins to the priest, we are confessing them to Christ, and Christ forgives us.

Because they serve as ministers of Christ, priests should show people the kindness and mercy of Jesus. Most priests realize this and act accordingly. However, priests are human; they can fail to show Christ's kindness to penitents, just as parents can fail to show Christ's love to their children. Penitents who encounter a priest seriously lacking in compassion should pray for that priest, but they should also seek out another confessor.

Priests may never reveal what they have been told in confession. This "seal of confession" assures penitents that what they say in confession will never be disclosed or used against them in any way.

Sometimes people worry, "What will Father think of me if I confess this or that sin?" Father is a sinner, just as the apostles were sinners, and Father goes to confession too. If a priest looks down on a penitent, he is committing a terrible sin of pride, worse than anything that might have been confessed to him. Further, confessors hear every sin imaginable, and nothing they are told will shock them. Most priests would agree with this statement of an experienced confessor: "When people confess sins they think especially shameful, I don't look down on them, but respect them for their courage and honesty."

Miracle and Privilege

Maybe we wouldn't, like the little second grader, call the sacrament of Penance "fun." (Admitting our faults is seldom fun.) But it is a miracle to be able to confess our sins to Christ, present through the priest, and to hear Christ say, "Your sins are forgiven. Go in peace." It is a privilege to be part of a Church which has accepted this sacrament as a gift from Christ and celebrated it for almost two thousand years.

Questions for Discussion and Reflection

When you go to confession, do you try consciously to realize that you are really confessing your sins to Christ, and that Christ is the one who is telling you that your sins are forgiven?

What is your favorite gospel passage displaying Christ's mercy and compassion? Do you remember when you go to confession that Christ looks upon you with such mercy and compassion?

Consider this statement: "Christ wants to forgive us even more than we want to be forgiven." Is it true or false? Why?

Activities

Sometimes we harbor bad feelings toward others because they have harmed us in some serious way. At other times, we let the little idiosyncrasies and bad habits of others "get on our nerves." Spend a few minutes talking to Jesus about any ill feelings you may be fostering against others. Say this little prayer: "Jesus, please give me *your* attitude toward...."

CHAPTER NINE
Catholic Prayer

A t Catholic funeral services, a rosary may be placed in the hands of the deceased. This custom says much about Catholic prayer and of how it joins us to God in life and in death. Traditionally, Catholic prayer involves both body and spirit. It binds the lives of those who pray to the historical life of Christ, and it foreshadows our eternal destiny, union with Christ in heaven.

Liturgical Prayer

The rosary is distinctively Catholic. The most important Catholic prayer, however, is not the rosary, but liturgical prayer, the "official prayer" of the Church. This includes the Mass, the celebration of the sacraments, Benediction, the Liturgy of the Hours, and liturgical blessings (which will be explained in Chapter Ten).

Liturgical prayer is a powerful expression of the sacramental principle. In the gathering of a congregation, in the readings of Scripture, and in the prayers and sacred gestures of worship, Christ enters our world and unites himself to us. At the sacred liturgy, Christ associates the Church with himself in giving perfect praise to God and making human beings holy. "From this it follows that every liturgical celebration, because it is an action of Christ the priest and of His Body the Church, is a sacred action surpassing all others" (SVC, *Liturgy*, 7).

There is nothing we do on this earth that is more important than our participation in the liturgy. It is possible to forget this, however, and we need often to reflect on what is really happening and on who is truly present at every liturgical celebration.

People will go to extreme lengths to see a famous politician or military hero, to get an autograph from a celebrity, or to attend a concert by a popular singer. But at every liturgical celebration, Jesus Christ, the Son of God and the greatest human being who ever lived, is present! He is present to join us with one another as members of his Body. He is present, not as some aloof dignitary, but as one who enters our lives and hearts to give each of us a personal audience.

To understand this is to realize the possibilities for communal and personal prayer at every celebration of the liturgy. Prayer is communication with God the Father, Son, and Holy Spirit. Prayer is listening as God addresses us, and then responding to God as a community and as individuals. God speaks to us in many ways through the liturgy, but above all in the words of Scripture. We respond to God in spoken words, in song, and in gestures.

"But in order that the sacred liturgy may produce its full effect, it is necessary that the faithful come to it with proper dispositions, that their thoughts match their words, and that they cooperate with divine grace....[and] take part knowingly, actively, and fruitfully" (SVC, *Liturgy*, 11).

The Mass as Prayer

We have already studied the Mass as a meal and as a sacrifice. Here we focus on the Mass as prayer, as communication with God. Every part of the Mass is prayer, and if we heed the instruction of the Second Vatican Council and match our thoughts with our words, we will appreciate the Mass more and more as a special time of communicating with God.

There are four basic kinds of prayer: adoration, thanksgiving, sorrow, and petition. The various parts of the Mass will always fit into one or more of these categories. At Mass, then, we praise God, thank God for the blessings God bestows on us (*Eucharist* means "giving thanks" or "gratitude"), seek forgiveness from God, and ask God for what we and others need.

Mass often begins with a hymn; different parts of the Mass may be sung, and other hymns and sacred music may form part of our eucharistic celebration. Saint Augustine said that singing is praying twice—through the words and the music. We must, therefore, view singing not as a "performance," but as prayer. We should make a conscious effort to heed the meaning of the words and to address them to God.

A kind of prayer used often at Mass, but sometimes not perceived as prayer, is the pattern of responses said by the congregation. The priest says, "The Lord be with you," and the congregation responds, "And also with you." These words are more than friendly greetings; they are prayers asking God to be in those we address. "Lord, have mercy" is a prayer asking God for forgiveness. "Thanks be to God" and "Praise to you, Lord Jesus Christ" are prayers of gratitude to God for speaking to us in the Scriptures. "Blessed be God forever" is praise and thanks. *Amen* is a Hebrew word, a prayer meaning "So be it," or, more personally, "I proclaim my belief in this truth." *Alleluia* is another Hebrew expression which means "Praise the Lord."

The postures we take at Eucharist should be prayer. When we stand, we are not just "standing around" as we might in a lobby; we are taking an ancient posture of prayer, addressing God as the Source of all good things. When we sit, we are not just taking a comfortable position as we might at a theater; rather, we are placing ourselves in an attentive attitude to hear God's Word. When we kneel, genuflect, or bow, we are expressing humble adoration before the Lord, who is truly present among us. Gestures are "sacramental prayers," physical signs of inward dispositions of worship.

We can easily recognize certain parts of the Mass as prayer. The Opening Prayer, Prayer Over the Gifts, and Prayer After Communion are identified by their titles. "I confess" is obviously a prayer of sorrow. "Glory to God in the highest" is a prayer of praise. The Responsorial Psalm is a prayer of meditation on the first reading from Scripture. "We believe in one God" is an expression of our belief and a prayer for stronger faith. The General Intercessions place before God the needs of the Church and the world. The Eucharistic Prayers are praise, thanksgiving, remembering, union, love, petition. The Lord's Prayer is unique in that it was given to us by Jesus himself. The "Deliver us" and prayer for peace allow us to place our desires for personal and world peace before God. Yes, we easily recognize these as prayers, but we must work at being attentive to them. We should frequently ask for the aid of the Holy Spirit, who "helps us to pray as we ought" (Romans 8:26).

The Other Sacraments as Prayer

We have all been to baptisms and confirmations, celebrated the weddings of friends, and attended funeral Masses of departed relatives. Perhaps we have been to communal services of the sacrament of Penance, witnessed the ordination of an acquaintance to the priesthood, or been present when a loved one was anointed. Even when we realize that these events are liturgical acts where Christ is among us in a unique way, we can forget that they are also special times for prayer.

They are, and they actualize the sacramental principle in powerful and dramatic ways through the signs which are an essential part of each celebration. We are called, as Catholics, to be attentive to the spiritual realities made present by the signs and to participate actively at each celebration of the sacraments. We are never mere observers.

We may attend a wedding because we are invited and because we want to share our friends' joy. But we are also privileged to pray for those friends, and our active participation can help open them to the blessings only Christ can give. We may be present at a funeral out of respect for the deceased and to show our love for the family. But as Catholics, we pray for the deceased, and our prayers can help escort the deceased from this life to the happiness of heaven. At baptisms and confirmations we pray that those receiving the sacraments may be receptive to the grace of Baptism and Confirmation, not only as the water is being poured or the oil bestowed but for all the days of their lives. At communal Penance services, we pray for pardon and peace, not only for ourselves, but for the whole community. At ordinations, we are present as members of the community calling the new deacon or priest or bishop to be faithful to the holy order granted by Christ. At an anointing of the sick, we are there to bring the sick person to Christ, in imitation of those in the gospels who brought their friends to him (Mark 1:32-34; 2:1-12). At each celebration of the sacraments, we are present as members of Christ's Body. We are signs through whom Christ is present and in whom Christ intercedes for the world. We offer our own lives and our own prayers on earth in union with the offering and prayer of Christ in heaven.

Benediction and Adoration of the Blessed Sacrament

Christ's Real Presence in the Eucharist derives from the fact that Christ himself changes the bread and wine into his own body and blood. For this reason, the Catholic Church preserves the Blessed Sacrament in tabernacles in churches or chapels so that Holy Communion may be available to the sick, and the faithful may adore Christ truly present in the Eucharist.

The Church highly recommends public and private devotion to the Holy Eucharist outside Mass. The most common public devotion is exposition of the Blessed Sacrament with Benediction, and this is also an act of liturgical worship. The consecrated host is placed on the altar in a monstrance (a sacred vessel in which the host may be seen). The Scriptures are read, prayers are said, hymns are sung, and some time is devoted to silent prayer. Adoration may be expressed by the use of incense. Then the congregation is blessed with the Holy Sacrament, and the liturgical service concludes with prayers and a hymn. This devotion, of course, is a clear demonstration of our faith in the Real Presence, and it nourishes and strengthens that faith.

Catholics are also encouraged to make "visits" to the Blessed Sacrament. Some people frequently "drop in" at Catholic churches just to say hello to the Lord. Some have the practice of frequently making a "holy hour," spending time in the Lord's presence reading the Bible and talking with Christ. Many parishes have instituted the practice of perpetual adoration, wherein the Blessed Sacrament is venerated constantly by people who take turns so that someone is always present before the Lord.

All such adoration of the Blessed Sacrament should be in harmony with the celebration of the Mass and should attract people to the Liturgy of the Mass. Eucharistic devotion thus reminds us of the Incarnation and of our redemption through the life, death, and resurrection of Jesus Christ, and it is a constant reminder of God's way of dealing with humanity through signs which God has created.

The Liturgy of the Hours

One of the fundamentals of the sacramental principle is that we find God in the everyday deeds and hourly routines which make up our lives. From New Testament times to the present, the Church has exemplified this reality by recommending that its members discover God in ordinary actions and unite those actions to God in patterns of prayer throughout the day. The New Testament speaks of the apostles praying at various times (Acts 1:1-15; 3:1; 10:9; 16:25), and gradually the Church came to celebrate prayer throughout the day in the Liturgy of the Hours, also called the Divine Office.

As now prayed by priests, deacons, religious, and many laypeople, the Liturgy of the Hours consists of five "hours" or times for prayer. These are the office of readings, morning prayer, midday prayer, evening prayer, and night prayer. Each includes psalms, Scripture readings, and intercessions. Variety is provided by a four-week cycle of the hours, as well as by a calendar of feasts following the Church year.

Some parishes invite members to communal recitation of parts of the Liturgy of the Hours, especially morning and evening prayer. Some laypeople recite the entire Office each day, and others recite one or another part. "...when this wonderful song of praise is worthily rendered by priests and others who are deputed for this purpose by Church ordinance, or by the faithful praying together with the priests in an approved form...it is the very prayer which Christ Himself, together with His body, addresses to the Father" (SVC, *Liturgy*, 84), and therefore is part of the liturgical prayer of the Church.

One feature of the Liturgy of the Hours is especially deserving of our attention: its frequent use of the Old Testament Book of Psalms. The Book of Psalms is of great importance to Catholics, even for those who do not pray the Divine Office. Catholics recite portions of the psalms at every Mass and at many other liturgical functions. And the Book of Psalms is a significant resource for private prayer for all Catholics.

The Book of Psalms is a collection of one hundred fifty prayers in the form of Hebrew poetry. The psalms were written more than two thousand years ago for Jews. Yet, they have been prayed by believers of every age, nation, and culture, and they remain popular today.

The psalms are "sacramental" in that they deal largely with human feelings and give us words to express our emotions to God. Being general in tone, they allow us to fit our particular circumstances into their framework. The psalms thus show that the emotional side of human nature is an integral part of our relationship with God. They are sacramental also in that they allow us to stand before God, not as isolated individuals but as members of the Catholic community of believers who have prayed them through the centuries and who pray with us today.

The psalms do present some difficulties, however. The thoughts do not always flow smoothly, and the poetry of the psalms is not based on rhyme or meter. Instead, Hebrew poetry depends on the balance of ideas. The Jews developed their poetry by establishing certain patterns of thought, and when we become aware of these patterns, we will better appreciate the "music" of the psalms.

The most common pattern is *repetition*, where similar ideas are expressed in different words:

> Hear my words, O Lord,
>> listen to my sighing (Psalm 5:2).

Another pattern frequently used is *contrast*, where dissimilar ideas are compared:

> No one is disgraced who waits for you,
>> but only those who lightly break faith (Psalm 25:3).

A third pattern may be called *construction*; here, ideas are built upon one another:

> Lord, your love reaches to heaven;
>> your fidelity, to the clouds.
> Your justice is like the highest mountains;
>> your judgments, like the mighty deep;
>> all living creatures you sustain, Lord.
> (Psalm 36:6-7)

Knowing these patterns, we can enjoy the flow and balance of ideas in Hebrew poetry and more readily understand and appreciate the psalms.

It is often helpful to adapt the psalms to our own situation. For example, Psalm 23 will have one meaning for a person setting out on a long journey, another to someone waiting for the results of a medical test.

The psalms can be powerful intercessory prayers, especially when we pray them for another as if we were that other person. In praying Psalm 6, for instance, we may not be feeling the distress and anguish verbalized in the psalm, but we may know a friend who is experiencing pain and sorrow. We can pray Psalm 6 in the name of that friend, who through our prayer can be touched by God's grace.

A good way to adapt the psalms to our own prayer life is to read through them and make a list of those which are meaningful for private or family prayer. Laypeople are also encouraged to use the Liturgy of the Hours. The entire four-volume set is available at Catholic bookstores. Most Catholic bookstores also have abbreviated versions which can be very helpful for Catholics who want to be a part of the official daily prayer of the Church. "...all who perform this service are not only fulfilling a duty of the Church but also are sharing in the greatest honor accorded to Christ's spouse, for by offering these praises to God they are standing before God's throne in the name of the Church their Mother" (SVC, *Liturgy*, 85).

Other Forms of Catholic Prayer

Liturgical prayer is the official prayer of the Church, but Catholics have a rich tradition of other prayers stretching back over nineteen centuries. Among the prayers most familiar to Catholics today are the Sign of the Cross, Our Father, Hail Mary, Glory (Prayer of Praise), and Apostles' Creed. Many Catholics also memorize Acts of Faith, Hope, Love, Contrition, and a form of grace before meals.

There are many kinds of Catholic prayer books, like those given to children making their first Holy Communion or the well-worn books seen in the hands of the elderly. Typical Catholic prayer books will offer prayers for every situation in life, as well as useful patterns for putting our feelings and ideas into words.

The rosary, mentioned in the opening part of this chapter, shows that prayer is a matter of the body, as well as of the spirit. We are flesh and blood, and we communicate with our whole being. The rosary with its cross, chain, and beads is something we can see and touch. The vocal prayers of the rosary involve our voice and our hearing. The words we repeat remind us that Mary and the saints are one with us in prayer. The mysteries of the rosary bind our lives to the historical life of Christ and foreshadow our eternal destiny, union with Christ in heaven. Saying the rosary with others reminds us of the importance of praying with the community of believers. And while the rosary is a Catholic prayer, it is loved and prayed by many who are not Catholic. A recent book praising the rosary, *Five for Sorrow, Ten for Joy* (Cowley Publications), was written by a Methodist minister, J. Neville Ward.

Another Catholic prayer clearly involving body and spirit is the Way of the Cross. Most Catholic churches have stations of the cross, traditional scenes from the passion and death of Christ. Catholics may walk from station to station, following in the footsteps of Christ, praying in their own words or from a formula. Many parishes schedule times for praying the Stations of the Cross in common during the season of Lent.

Litanies are forms of Catholic prayer usually said in common. In litanies, a leader speaks or sings a series of petitions or invocations (such as a list of saints or a list of titles for Christ or Mary), and the community answers with a set response (such as "Pray for us" or "Lord, hear our prayer"). Probably the best known litany is the Litany of the Saints, calling upon many saints by name to pray for us and listing needs and requests. This litany is used in whole or in part in some liturgical services, and several other litanies have been approved by the Church for public use, most notably the Litany of Loreto of the Blessed Virgin Mary.

The repetition involved in the rosary, in litanies, and in some other Catholic prayers has sometimes drawn condemnation from those hostile to the Church. They say that Matthew 6:8 forbids the repetition of prayers. However, all modern Protestant and Catholic translations of this passage show that Jesus is not condemning repetition in itself, but the use of empty, meaningless words. Jesus is telling us not to babble prayers without attending to their meaning. He is condemning the "pagan" notion that God can be coerced by incantations. He is not forbidding the meaningful repetition of prayer, for he himself repeated prayers during his agony in the garden (Matthew 26:36-44), and he encouraged us to persevere in prayer (Luke 11:5-8). Further, the Bible itself includes inspired prayers, like Psalm 136, which use "litanylike" refrains. Repetitive prayer, if said with thought and feeling, has a special power to attune us to God and to spiritual realities.

Mental Prayer

The Catholic Church teaches that God's creation is good and that people, things, and events reveal God's goodness and love. The Church teaches also that we have been given a share in the life of God, and that we are called to an intimate union with God here on earth, as well as in eternity. To appreciate these facts and to internalize them, Catholics need to reflect on spiritual realities and on how they are manifested to us. We must meditate on the Real Presence of Jesus in the Blessed Sacrament, for example, if we are to value this miracle as we ought. Mental prayer is reflection on spiritual realities, and it has long been honored in the Catholic Church.

The Church recommends mental prayer to all its members. "Only by the light of faith and by meditation on the word of God can one always and everywhere recognize God in whom 'we live, and move, and have our being' (Acts 17:28), seek His will in every event, see Christ in all men whether they be close to us or strangers, and make correct judgments about the true meaning and value of temporal things, both in themselves and in relation to man's final goal" (SVC, *Laity*, 4).

There are many different kinds of mental prayer. One of the best known is a type of meditation taught by Saint Ignatius of Loyola. After directing our attention to God, we consider, for instance, some incident from the gospels. We place ourselves at the scene, imagining the sights and sounds. We talk with Jesus. We make some practical resolution.

Another method of mental prayer is reflective reading, wherein we read from the Bible or a spiritual book, pausing to think and pray each time some passage inspires us. Another is the Jesus Prayer, where we gently pray the name of Jesus and remain aware of his presence and love.

Imaging prayer is a form of mental prayer which is built on images rather than words. We praise God by picturing ourselves kneeling before the throne of God in heaven. We thank God by visualizing the blessings we have received as gifts flowing from

God. We express sorrow for sin by mentally standing at the cross of Jesus. We make petitions by forming images of our needs and putting them before God. We pray for others by picturing Jesus standing next to them, placing his hands on them and blessing them. Imaging prayer is a beautiful way to end our day. After retiring, we visualize Jesus standing watch over people who need his help and over ourselves as we sleep.

Centering prayer is a focusing of one's heart, mind, and soul on God. This and similar forms of mental prayer are simple and contemplative: we place ourselves before God in silence, content just to be with the Lord. And this is really the purpose of all Catholic prayer: to fix our attention on God, to see God in everything good, to allow Christ to enter our hearts so that we can become Christ and say with Saint Paul, "I live, no longer I, but Christ lives in me" (Galatians 2:20).

Prayer First and Last

A tiny infant is welcomed into the prayer life of the Church through the sacrament of Baptism. An elderly person is ushered by the funeral liturgy into the prayer life of the saints in heaven. From first to last, we pray as members of the Church. From first to last, we are privileged to share in the prayer of the Church, which is the prayer of Christ.

Questions for Discussion and Reflection

Have you always seen the Mass and the sacraments as prayer? When attending Mass, have you appreciated the "Amen" and the other responses as true prayer? Do you think that Mass could ever be boring if people genuinely tried to "match their thoughts with their words" in every single prayer at Mass? What can we do to be more conscious of the fact that "every liturgical celebration is an action of Christ the priest" and to remember our union with Christ at every liturgical celebration?

What is your favorite way of praying? Why? What kind of prayer do you find most difficult? Why?

Activities

Take out your Bible, and turn to the Book of Psalms. Scan a few verses, and try to find examples of repetition, contrast, and construction.

Find a favorite psalm, and pray it reverently. Then think of a friend or relative in need; find a psalm which suits that person's situation and pray it in the name of that person.

Pray the rosary, applying each mystery first to some situation in your own life, then to a situation in the life of someone you know.

CHAPTER TEN
Catholic Sacramentals

I once heard a story about a little girl who had been invited to visit her grandparents on their farm. In the backyard was a birdbath, and one morning the grandmother observed the girl examining it with a puzzled look on her face. She walked around it once or twice, then dipped her finger into the water and made the Sign of the Cross!

It is characteristic of Catholics to find grace in ordinary things, and I'm sure that God smiled at the child's prayer. Even though the water wasn't blessed, it was good, for water is part of God's creation. And her prayer, the Sign of the Cross, was one of those especially good things we Catholics call "sacramentals."

Sacramentals

Sacramentals have long been a part of Catholic life, and they still are, as the Second Vatican Council taught in the third chapter of its *Constitution on the Sacred Liturgy*. Sacramentals are sacred signs which resemble the seven sacraments, but they are not instituted by Christ, and they do not convey Christ's grace in the same way the sacraments do. Instead, they are instituted by the Church and symbolize spiritual effects which come about primarily through the prayer of the Church. In a special way, sacramentals dispose us to receive the grace of the sacraments and sanctify various occasions in human life. (See SVC, *Liturgy*, 60.)

As a result of their connection to the prayer of the Church, the sacramentals open us to God's grace in ways that surpass personal prayer. When we use the sacramentals of the Church, we are, in a manner that is mysterious yet real, beneficiaries of the graces bestowed upon the Church by Jesus Christ. Our prayerful use of the sacramentals becomes a part of, and is enhanced by, the worship of the whole Church. Of course, we must approach the sacramentals with faith and devotion in order to be properly disposed to receive God's graces.

There are two main classifications of sacramentals: prayers of blessing and blessed objects. The child's Sign of the Cross was a sacramental prayer of blessing, and holy water (often kept in fonts which may resemble birdbaths!) is an example of a blessed object.

Prayers of Blessing: "Bless You!" "Bless the Lord!"

The word *bless* can have many meanings. It may mean to grant some favor or gift (as when God blesses us with life and grace). It may mean to ask God, through prayer and ritual, to sanctify and show favor to someone or to make something holy (as when we bless someone with the words, "God bless you"; this kind of blessing is also called a benediction). It may mean to honor as holy by praising or glorifying (as when we "bless the Lord").

All good things come from God, the source of every favor and gift. Therefore, the blessing prayers of the Church "bless" people or things by invoking God's grace and sanctification upon them. The prayers "bless" God with words of praise and thanks.

Both kinds of blessing prayers are found throughout the Bible. The best known of Old Testament prayers asking God's blessing on people has been traditionally called the blessing of Aaron: "The LORD bless you and keep you! The LORD let his face shine upon you, and be gracious to you! The LORD look upon you kindly and give you peace!" (Numbers 6:24-26) An ancient blessing of people and objects is the blessing of Moses: "May you be blessed in the city, and blessed in the country! Blessed be the fruit of your womb, the produce of your soil and the offspring of your livestock, the issue of your herds and the young of your flocks! Blessed be your grain bin and your kneading bowl! May you be blessed in your coming in, and blessed in your going out!" (Deuteronomy 28:3-6) There are many Old Testament blessing prayers that praise God. A good example is Psalm 103, whose first verse is an enthusiastic invitation to glorify God: "Bless the LORD, O my soul; and all my being, bless his holy name."

In the New Testament, Jesus blessed both people and things; he blessed the little children (Mark 10:17) and he blessed food (Luke 9:16). There are many New Testament prayers which "bless" God. The Canticle of Zechariah praises God for the gift of salvation: "Blessed be the Lord, the God of Israel, for he has visited and brought redemption to his people" (Luke 1:68). Saint Paul often "blesses" God in his letters, praising God for favoring us: "Blessed be the God and Father of our Lord Jesus Christ, who has blessed us in Christ with every spiritual blessing in the heavens" (Ephesians 1:3-6).

Down through the centuries, the Church has followed the patterns of Scripture in offering prayers of blessing. Most official blessings used in the Church today may be found in the liturgical *Book of Blessings*, revised by decree of the Second Vatican Council and published in the United States in 1989. This book is a real treasury of prayers and blessings for all Catholics.

The *Book of Blessings*

The *Book of Blessings* is a clear expression of Catholic belief in the sacramental principle. The Church, in its prayers of praise and blessing, demonstrates its conviction that "there is hardly any proper use of material things that cannot thus be directed toward human sanctification and the praise of God" (*Book of Blessings*, General Introduction, 14).

Because the prayers in the *Book of Blessings* are part of the Church's liturgy, they should ordinarily be used in a communal celebration. Some blessings, like those of religious articles and those connected to a diocesan or parish function, must be celebrated by a bishop, priest, or deacon. But most liturgical blessings given apart from a church may be celebrated by any Catholic in virtue of Christ's universal priesthood, shared through the sacraments of Baptism and Confirmation.

Liturgical blessings follow a typical pattern. After a brief introduction and opening prayer, there is a reading from sacred Scripture followed by a responsorial psalm. Next come General Intercessions, to which may be added special intentions of the participants. The prayer of blessing is then said, accompanied by some outward sign such as the raising of hands, the laying on of hands, the Sign of the Cross, sprinkling with holy water, or the use of incense. The liturgy closes with a brief concluding rite.

This structure allows those who are present to join in the celebration of the blessing. In a family blessing of a Christmas tree, for example, the father might give the introduction and proclaim the readings, the children offer the Intercessions, and the mother say the blessing. In most cases, there are alternate short blessing forms available, but even in their longer forms, the prayers of blessing take only a few minutes and are so designed that small children can participate.

There are two English editions of the *Book of Blessings* approved for use in the United States. The first contains all the liturgical blessings of the Church. The second is a shorter edition which omits the blessings to be celebrated at church. This shorter edition is the more suitable of the two for laypeople, and it should find an honored place in every Catholic home. It can be obtained at most Catholic bookstores.

Becoming Familiar With the *Book of Blessings*

The *Book of Blessings* begins with a General Introduction, which offers a fine explanation of blessing prayers in the history of salvation and of the Church. It explains that "blessings are signs that have God's word as their basis and that are celebrated from motives of faith...signs above all of spiritual effects that are achieved through the Church's intercession" (10). It notes that when there is a blessing of objects or places, this is always done "with a view to the people who use the objects to be blessed and frequent the places to be blessed" (12). In other words, the purpose of all blessings is to sanctify people, to help them grow in holiness and in their desire and ability to serve and worship God.

The first main division of the complete book, Part One, contains blessings directly pertaining to persons. Here are found blessings of families, of engaged and married couples, of children, of parents before and after childbirth, of those celebrating a birthday, of the elderly, of the sick, of students and teachers, and of travelers. There are special blessings for particular circumstances, such as blessings for parents after a miscarriage, for parents of an adopted child, for people suffering from addiction or substance abuse, and for victims of crime.

Part Two has blessings related to buildings and to various forms of human activity. There are blessings for homes and many other kinds of structures, blessings for automobiles, boats, tools and equipment, blessings for animals, for fields and flocks, for planting and harvest, and for athletic events. There are several forms of blessings to be used before and after meals.

Part Three includes blessings for objects designed to be used in churches, such as baptismal fonts, lecterns, tabernacles, bells, organs, and stations of the cross. There are also blessings of sacred items, like chalices and patens, of holy water, and of cemeteries.

Part Four offers blessings for religious articles such as rosaries, scapulars, and medals.

Part Five contains blessings related to feasts and seasons of the Church. Some of these, like Advent wreaths, nativity scenes, and Christmas trees, are especially suitable for family celebrations. There are blessings of homes at Christmas and Easter, of throats for Saint Blaise Day, of ashes for Ash Wednesday, of food for special occasions, of mothers for Mother's Day, and of fathers for Father's Day. There is also a rite of blessing for visiting cemeteries on All Souls' Day, Memorial Day, and on anniversaries.

Part Six contains blessings for pastoral ministers, readers, altar servers, sacristans, musicians, ushers, parish-council members, lay ministers, and officers of parish societies. It offers blessings to welcome new parishioners and to say good-bye to those who are leaving, blessings for those receiving ecclesiastical honors and for inaugurating public officials. There are general blessings for giving thanks and for asking God to bless people, things, and events not specifically designated elsewhere in the book.

Finally, there are appendices which contain blessing prayers for the installation of a new pastor, and the solemn blessings and prayers found in *The Roman Missal*. These may be used to conclude any of the other blessings, or on any occasion when a priest or deacon is asked to give a blessing.

Blessings Are a Blessing!

Most Catholics make the Sign of the Cross and say the traditional "Bless us, O Lord, and these thy gifts" before meals. But they may not be fully aware of their privilege and right, through Baptism and Confirmation, to offer other blessings.

Carol Ann started blessing her children every night when they were quite small. This became a family tradition which expanded to include friends of the children who also wanted to be blessed. The custom has continued now that the children have grown up, with family members often saying prayers of blessing for one another. They feel that their prayers of blessing have been truly "life-transforming."

Hopefully, many other Catholics will be inspired by the *Book of Blessings* to imitate Carol Ann and her family in their frequent use of blessing prayers. Its riches can only be hinted at in this brief summary, but Catholics who use the book regularly will find their prayer life enhanced. They will grow in their appreciation of the sacramental principle and of God's presence in their lives.

Sacramental Objects

Jesus gave his Church the sacraments, outward signs of inward grace. The water of Baptism, the oil of Confirmation and Anointing of the Sick, the bread and wine of the Eucharist, and all the other signs of the sacraments inspired the Church to appreciate the goodness of material things and their ability to signify spiritual realities. As a consequence, the Church has designated many other signs as sacramentals, blessed objects which bear some resemblance to the sacraments.

Sacramentals and Sacraments

Most sacramentals are related to the sacraments. Thus, holy water is water that is blessed to remind us of our Baptism. When we dip our fingers in holy water and make the Sign of the Cross, blessing ourselves, we are reminded of our Baptism in the name of the Father, Son, and Holy Spirit. As the water of Baptism sanctifies those who receive it, so holy water is sprinkled on people and objects to call God's blessing upon them.

At the Easter Vigil service, a large candle is lit to symbolize the Resurrection of Christ from the darkness of the grave. This paschal candle is used in the blessing of the water for baptisms at the Easter Vigil. At every baptism, a blessed candle is lit from the paschal candle to symbolize that Christ's life and light are granted to the baptized.

At Baptism, a white garment is placed on those baptized. This garment is an important symbol to all Christians that we are clothed with Christ. But the rituals of Baptism and the white garment have a particular significance for men and women who join religious communities. The blessings and ceremonies associated with consecration to religious life flow from the rituals of Baptism. The habits and special garb worn by many religious are outward expressions of how they "put on the Lord Jesus Christ" (Romans 13:14) through the vows of religious life.

Laypeople who have some affiliation with religious communities may express this through the use of scapulars. These are small squares of cloth worn around the neck to symbolize one's association with a religious community or membership in a spiritual organization. Blessed medals sometimes substitute for scapulars, and they may be seen as a special sign of baptismal commitment to Jesus Christ, or of devotion to Mary or one of the saints.

Blessed oils are related to our baptismal identification with Christ. *Christ* means "Anointed One," and the anointings at Baptism symbolize the fact that we are members of the Body of Christ.

The oils used in celebrations of the sacraments are usually blessed by the bishop of a diocese on Holy Thursday. The oil of catechumens is used at Baptism and in the Rite of Christian Initiation of Adults. Sacred chrism (perfumed oil) is used at Baptism, Confirmation, Holy Orders, and for some blessings. The oil of the sick draws its symbolism of healing from oil-based medicines and is used at the Anointing of the Sick. The *Book of Blessings* offers a blessing of oil to be used apart from the sacraments as a symbol of God's grace and healing power.

Church buildings are blessed for the celebration of the Eucharist and the other sacraments. At Mass, candles symbolize the light of Christ, and a sanctuary light reminds us that Christ is present in the Blessed Sacrament. Blessed candles and votive (prayer) lights are related to the Eucharist, as well as to Baptism, reminding Catholics that Christ is "the light of the world" (John 8:12). Incense, which is blessed with a silent Sign of the Cross, may express our adoration at the Eucharist and at some other liturgical services. Church bells, which are blessed to call people to worship, are thereby related to the Eucharist. Crosses, crucifixes, and the stations of the cross call to mind the saving death of Christ made present in the Eucharist. On Passion Sunday, palms are blessed at a celebration of the Eucharist; they remind us of Christ's willingness to accept death on the cross to save us.

On Ash Wednesday, palms from the previous year are burned; the ashes are then blessed and used to sign the faithful in the form of a cross as a call to repentance. This signing with blessed ashes is related to the sacrament of Penance.

Wedding rings, which are blessed and exchanged at celebrations of the sacrament of Matrimony, are sacramentals, beautiful signs of love and commitment. Being made of precious metal, they are reminders of the pricelessness of God's love. Being circular in form, they remind us that human love originates in the love of God, which has existed from all eternity and will endure forever.

Many of the sacramentals already mentioned are used again at funerals. For example, the paschal candle is placed in a prominent location, expressing our belief that Christ rose from the dead to bring us to eternal life. A white pall, recalling the baptismal garment, is placed on the casket in recognition of the deceased person's efforts to put on Christ. The Eucharist, with its ceremonies and sacramentals, makes present the death and resurrection of Christ. It reminds the faithful that Christ is the bread of life and that those who believe in him will live forever (John 6:48-51).

Other sacramentals, such as rosaries, statues, and sacred images, are at least implicitly connected to the sacraments, for they remind us of the supernatural life given us by Christ. The rosary binds us to Mary, who lived in the grace of her son and who now watches over us, her children. Statues and sacred images direct our attention to the saints, who are our models in faithfulness to the life of grace given us at Baptism. These, and all sacramental objects, dispose us to "receive the chief effect of the sacraments, and various occasions in life are rendered holy" (SVC, *Liturgy*, 60).

Making Use of the Sacramentals

Blessings and the use of material things as signs of God's presence and power are elements of Catholicism that have their foundation in Scripture. Jesus, as we have seen, blessed people and things. He instructed his apostles to anoint the sick with oil, and he used mud and saliva to cure a blind man. The Acts of the Apostles describes how the first Christians used sacramental signs to bring Christ's grace and healing to people: "So extraordinary were the mighty deeds God accomplished at the hands of Paul that when face cloths or aprons that touched his skin were applied to the sick, their diseases left them and the evil spirits came out of them" (Acts 19:11-12).

Inspired by Jesus and by the testimony of Scripture, the Catholic Church has recommended the use of sacramentals as additional signs of God's care for us. Catholics have embraced sacramentals with enthusiasm because they fit into our natural human inclination to use material things as symbols of profound realities. A gift of flowers is a sign that conveys love and can help love grow. A work of art can express powerful emotions and can elicit them from people who experience it. So, too, sacramentals express God's mighty power and convey God's grace to us through the intercession of the Church. For these and many other reasons, sacramentals are as important and "up to date" in our modern world as they have ever been.

In today's world, where secular signs abound and where materialism is promoted by the media, sacramentals declare the importance of spiritual realities. A cross or medal worn around the neck can prompt us to pray more often. Crucifixes and statues in the home tell of the presence of Christ and the communion of saints; they also proclaim to the world that this is a Catholic home. The use of holy water, blessed candles, and other sacramentals call to mind the sacraments we have received and the protection only God can give.

Obviously, sacramentals differ from magic incantations and superstitious good-luck charms. Incantations and charms are presumed to have a power of their own. Sacramentals derive their special value from the prayer of the Church, which ultimately is a participation in the prayer of Jesus Christ, the Son of God.

While certain objects, chiefly those we have mentioned above, are sacramentals, not every blessed object can be considered a sacramental. Only those objects which are in some way identified with the worship of the Church are true sacramentals. Thus, holy water is clearly a sacramental, as are all the other articles described as related to the sacraments and to worship.

Blessed objects not identified with worship do not become

sacramentals. When a pet is blessed, for example, it does not thereby become a sacramental. But the blessing shows pets are gifts that in some way reflect the goodness and creative power of God. In similar ways, all blessed objects, places, and events proclaim that the proper use of material things directs them to our eternal salvation and to God's glory. They call to mind the advice given by Saint Paul: "So whether you eat or drink, or whatever you do, do everything for the glory of God" (1 Corinthians 10:31).

Most sacramental blessings may be bestowed on anyone who desires them. Most sacramental objects may be used by anyone, Catholic or not, if the person has the proper dispositions of faith and openness to God's grace.

Indulgences

Indulgences are not sacramentals but are related to them because both are special ways in which Christ's grace is brought to us through the Church. An indulgence is a declaration by the Church that certain prayers or actions have special value because they bestow a sharing in the grace and merits of Christ. The word *indulgence* is not found in the Bible, but indulgences are based on the biblical teaching of Saint Paul that members of Christ's Body can help one another (1 Corinthians 12:12-27). Paul also shows that the merits of one member can be applied to others when he says: "...in my flesh I am filling up what is lacking in the afflictions of Christ on behalf of his body, which is the church" (Colossians 1:24). The use of indulgences, then, is a symbolic way of showing the worth of action and prayer made in the Church.

Sacramentals: Signs of God's Goodness and Love

The birdbath water which the little girl used to bless herself wasn't officially a sacramental. But water and all created things are gifts of God, made holy by the Incarnation of Jesus Christ. We, as Catholics, are privileged to be led by our understanding of sacramentals to a greater appreciation of the goodness of God's creation and of the power of Christ's redemptive love.

Questions for Discussion and Reflection

Before you read this chapter, were you aware that laypeople could give liturgical blessings? Have you ever seen or used the *Book of Blessings?* Which sacramentals are most important to you? Why? How many sacramental objects in your home can you name? (If you are married, don't forget your wedding ring!)

Catholics are sometimes criticized for using sacramentals as magic charms. Can you explain in your own words why and how sacramentals differ from magic?

Activities

Catholics are sometimes criticized because we display crucifixes which show the body of Christ on the cross. Of course, we believe that Christ is risen, but we want to remember Christ's love in dying for us. Look up the following Scripture passages and try to develop an explanation from the New Testament about why we honor crucifixes: 1 Corinthians 1:23; 1 Corinthians 2:2; Galatians 2:19-20; Galatians 3:1; Galatians 6:14; Colossians 1:24.

CHAPTER ELEVEN
The Communion of Saints

"Hunter watches over us," the young father said, "and I talk to him often. I know he hears me, and I feel close to him." Hunter, only two years old, had died in a tragic accident. Years later, his parents still experienced grief, but they also felt that Hunter was truly with them. He was their "angel," their "saint," as close to them after death as he had been in life.

Hunter's father is not Catholic, but his belief about the nearness of the saints to us is a belief that Catholics have held since the first Christians honored the martyrs and asked for their help. Catholics believe in the communion of saints, in the bond between us on earth and those who have died in Christ's grace. We believe that the saints watch over us and that we can pray to them, talking to them as friends and helpers.

Catholic Belief in the Saints

When we who are Catholic speak of the saints, we mean all who now enjoy the presence of God in heaven. In the earliest days of the Church, the apostles and martyrs were paid special honor. As the Church continued to grow, others who had led holy lives were revered in various places. In time, the Church developed a process called "canonization," in which people remarkable for their holiness were formally named saints. Today, the Catholic Church has a liturgical calendar of the saints, honoring those whose lives have a special importance for the whole Church. Many other saints are remembered in specific localities or by special groups. All those in heaven are honored as saints on All Saints' Day, November 1.

Saints and Cooperation With God's Grace

Not all Christians accept the reality of saints. Those who believe in extrinsic justification, in the theory that Christ covers over our sinfulness instead of taking away our sins, contend that all goodness must be credited to Christ, not to any human being. In this theory there can be no saints, because no one but Christ can do anything deserving of credit or praise.

We Catholics acknowledge that without God's grace we can do nothing good. But we believe that human beings have free wills and can choose either to cooperate with God's grace or to reject it. Saints are those who freely commit their lives to God and allow God's grace to transform them. Aided by the grace of God, they do good works, not as puppets on celestial strings but as free human beings who are praised for their accomplishments in heaven, as we see in the Book of Revelation. "Blessed are the dead who die in the Lord....Let them find rest from their labors, for their works accompany them" (14:13). The honor paid to the saints is symbolized as a white linen robe that clothes the Church, and "the linen represents the righteous deeds of the holy ones" (19:8).

Saints and the Sacramental Principle

If we could go back two thousand years and pay a visit to the Holy Family, would Jesus want us to ignore Mary and Joseph? Certainly not. Jesus would be pleased if we would visit with the whole family, and Mary and Joseph would inspire us to love Jesus more. Surely Jesus is pleased today when we visit not only with him but with Mary, Joseph, and the other members of his "holy family" in heaven.

If we could go back to Palestine and spend some time with Jesus and the twelve apostles, would Jesus forbid us to converse with the apostles? Of course not. Visiting with the apostles would fill us with their enthusiasm for the Lord and bring us closer to Jesus.

Christ is certainly pleased if we talk with the apostles today, and with the other saints who are close to him in heaven.

This understanding of the saints reflects the sacramental principle. Because we believe in the goodness of creation and of human beings, we trust that the saints will bring us closer to Jesus. Those, however, who do not honor the saints are afraid that somehow the saints will come between us and Jesus. They see the saints as obstacles, and they do not accept the sacramental principle that creation is meant to bring us to God.

We Catholics do not see the saints as obstacles. They are not a wall between us and Jesus, for we are "fellow citizens with the holy ones and members of the household of God, built upon the foundation of the apostles and prophets, with Christ Jesus as the capstone" (Ephesians 2:19-20). The saints do not take us away from Christ, but deepen our love of Christ and strengthen our devotion to him.

Saints and Our Catholic Understanding of Community

Some people do not honor the saints because they believe that each individual stands alone before Christ. We who are Catholic believe that Christian life is more than a matter of "me and Jesus." We do not relate to Christ as isolated individuals, but as members of the communion of saints. This expression, found in the Apostles' Creed, refers not only to the saints in heaven but to all people who are united with Christ, those in heaven, those on earth, and those in purgatory (about whom more will be said in Chapter Fifteen). God's plan is to "sum up all things in Christ, in heaven and on earth" (Ephesians 1:10). This Bible passage indicates a unity of heaven and earth brought about through Christ, not a unity of material objects, but a "community" among those who dwell in heaven and on earth.

Community is essential to us as human beings. We know how important it is for us to have friends here on earth. Loneliness is a burden that weighs heavily on people who feel isolated from others. Friends, relatives, and companions are blessings that bring warmth and joy into our lives.

Consider the case of two people in adjoining hospital rooms with the same illness. Both receive exactly the same medical treatment. But one has no visitors and no encouragement from family or friends. The other has plenty of visitors, gifts of flowers on the bedside table, and friendly greeting cards in the mail. The second person is almost certain to recover more quickly.

Consider also the "home-team advantage" spoken of in athletic competitions. To be surrounded by friends and supporters brings out the best in us, whether in sports or in life. The Bible tells us that we have the "home-team advantage." The Letter to the Hebrews compares life to a race we are running, with the heroes of the past, the saints, in the stands cheering us on. "Therefore, since we are surrounded by so great a cloud of witnesses, let us rid ourselves of every burden and sin that clings to us and persevere in running the race that lies before us" (12:1). With such evidence from Scripture and from human experience, it is sad that so many people think they must go through life without the companionship of the saints. It is sad that so many do not enjoy the advantages of our family ties with the saints.

Saints and Interaction
Between Heaven and Earth

Some people contend that those in heaven are not aware of us here on earth. But there are many clear indications in the Bible (in addition to Hebrews 12:1) that the saints in heaven are aware of us, and that there is interaction between those in heaven and us on earth. The Book of Revelation pictures the saints in heaven as offering to God the prayers of God's people on earth: "Each of the elders held a harp and gold bowls filled with incense, which are the prayers of the holy ones" (5:8). The Second Book of Maccabees 15:12-15 reports a vision in which the martyred high priest Onias and the prophet Jeremiah pray for the Jewish nation; even before the time of Christ there was a belief among Jews that saints are aware of earthly events and pray for us. The gospels portray Moses and Elijah appearing with Jesus at the transfiguration and talking with him about his coming passion and death (Luke 9:28-36). Jesus speaks of "joy in heaven over one sinner who repents" (Luke 15:7). Jesus reminds us of other "residents" of heaven who watch over us on earth: "See that you do not despise one of these little ones, for I say to you that their angels in heaven always look upon the face of my heavenly Father" (Matthew 18:10).

With such evidence of heavenly friends all around us, we have every reason to enjoy the companionship of the saints and angels. It is wonderful that Jesus Christ is our Lord and Savior. It is wonderful also that Christ offers us grace and salvation in the company of "a great multitude, which no one could count, from every nation, race, people, and tongue" (Revelation 7:9). We who are Catholic are privileged to know that we are members of the communion of saints and to offer this knowledge to all who believe in Jesus.

Catholic Prayer to the Saints

Catholics are sometimes asked, "Why do you pray to the saints? Why don't you go directly to Jesus?" We do, of course, pray directly to Jesus, but we also talk with the saints. It is important to note first of all that we do not pray to God and to the saints in the same way. We pray to God—Father, Son, and Holy Spirit—as the Source of all blessings. We pray to the saints in the sense that we ask them to pray with us and for us, to be near us in love and friendship, and to lead us closer to Jesus. This is illustrated in two prayers frequently said by Catholics. In the Lord's Prayer, we ask God for what only God can give: "Give us this day our daily bread, and forgive us our trespasses." In the Hail Mary, we ask Mary to "pray for us sinners."

Next, we must realize that we do not pray to the saints because we need them to persuade God to assist us. Rather, we pray to the saints because they help us open ourselves to the blessings God wants us to have. God knows what is best for us, but we may be prevented from receiving it because of our lack of faith, our own sins, or those of others. We may fail to know what is best for us because we do not perceive God's will or understand how it fits into our lives. The prayers of the saints open us to the will of God and make us more receptive to the graces God offers.

Finally, we ought to make the connection between asking people on earth to pray for us and asking the saints in heaven to pray for us. Jesus teaches us that there is a special value in praying with others: "For where two or three are gathered together in my name, there am I in the midst of them (Matthew 18:20). The Bible shows that we may request the prayers of others, as when Saint Paul asked believers to pray for him (Colossians 4:3;

1 Thessalonians 5:25). Paul prayed directly to God, but he also felt that it was important to have others praying with him and for him. If it is good to pray with others on earth and to ask them to pray for us, then it is also good to pray with the saints in heaven and to ask them to pray for us.

Honoring the Saints

No doubt you've seen the bumper sticker, "Ask us about our grandchildren." Go ahead and ask them! They'll tell you all about how wonderful their grandchildren are, and they'll have a pocketful of pictures to show you. It is human to praise the ones we love and to keep images and representations of them to remind us of them.

That is why Catholics have always honored the saints. We love them as family members who have gone before us, and we keep statues and paintings of them in our homes and churches. The statues and paintings, like pictures of grandchildren, are "sacramentals," that is, they are signs that bring the real person to mind. We Catholics value the signs and the saints they represent. Both flow from the sacramental principle. The goodness in both signs and saints enriches our lives and draws us closer to God.

Sometimes Catholics are criticized for "worshiping" the saints because we keep images of them and pray before those images. We do not, of course, "worship" the saints. We worship and adore God alone. But we do *honor* the saints. We remember their holy lives and we try to imitate them.

The Bible teaches us to do this: "Remember your leaders who spoke the word of God to you. Consider the outcome of their way of life and imitate their faith" (Hebrews 13:7). The Bible honors heroes and heroines of Old and New Testament times, in some cases with entire books like the Books of Ruth, Judith, and Esther. Surely, we are following the Bible when we memorialize and honor the saints in word and song, in marble, in stained glass, and on canvas.

As a matter of fact, most non-Catholic Christians erect statues of saints...at Christmastime when they put up nativity scenes with images of Mary and Joseph. We who are Catholic do not reserve the practice to Christmas; we have our statues all year-round. And there is really nothing unusual about keeping statues and paintings in prominent places. Almost any city in the world has its statues of great leaders and prominent citizens. Images of saints are signs of a special kind of greatness, dedication to Jesus Christ.

At times, Catholics may seem overly enthusiastic in their veneration of saints. But if we consider the kind of adulation commonly paid to movie stars, sports figures, and singers, we will probably have to admit that saints come in "second-best." The real problem is not that we honor the saints too much, but that we honor them too little.

Human beings will have their heroes and heroines, one way or another. If we, adults and children, are given only secular models to imitate, we will be denied the kind of models who can guide us to Jesus and to eternal life.

I grew up in the small town of Perryville, Missouri, and attended weekly Mass in a church built in the 1830s. Its walls are covered with paintings of martyrs and its altars populated with statues of saints. They are not masterpieces, but they taught me valuable lessons. They taught that many great people made Jesus Christ the Lord of their lives. They proclaimed Christ as a leader people would gladly die for. Statues of Saint Vincent de Paul and Saint Louise de Marillac spoke volumes about the importance of caring for the poor and needy. A painting of Mary's Assumption pointed to heaven as our final goal.

Statues and paintings are not false idols. They are signs of God's grace and goodness fleshed out in the lives of people very much like us. They are reminders that we are called to the only kind of greatness that matters, lives of dedication to Jesus Christ.

Patron Saints

Cities like San Francisco, Saint Louis, and San Antonio are so well known that we can forget they are named after patron saints. Santa Claus and Valentine Day have become so secularized that we can overlook their origins in the patron saints of giving and loving. Patron saints, in fact, have become so much a part of human existence that we take them for granted and need to reexamine their true meaning.

As far back as the fourth century, Christians named their children after apostles and martyrs. At about the same time, they began to dedicate churches to the honor of patron saints, often placing the church over the tombs of saints so honored. In time, not only churches but cities, nations, occupations, organizations, conditions, and even maladies were assigned patron saints, usually by popular acclaim, but occasionally through some official designation by the Church. Patron saints, then, are special helpers, guardians, models, and protectors.

Today, it is common for parents to give their child a patron saint's name at Baptism. Many young people choose a special patron at Confirmation. As mentioned above, many cities are named for patron saints, and customs relating to patron saints are part of our everyday life. Most people know of Saint Patrick, the patron saint of Ireland; Saint Joseph, the patron saint of carpenters; and Saint Anthony, the patron saint of lost articles.

Patron saints are invoked for special assistance and honored for their accomplishments. They remind us of the spiritual dimension of places, people, things, and situations. They serve as models for our imitation. They are positive indications of the sacramental principle, for they show that God can be found in every place, circumstance, and time. Saint Monica, the patron saint of mothers and wives, for example, is a sign that God is with parents even when their children go astray. Saint Isidore, the patron saint of farmers, reminds us that God strengthens us in our work and is pleased by humble tasks done well. Patron saints are signs of God's grace and presence, and they lead us to God.

All Saints

On November 1, the Church celebrates the feast of All Saints. This feast acknowledges that there are many in heaven who have not been officially recognized as saints by the Church. The feast invites us to remember our own saints, friends, and family members who have gone before us, and to ask them for their intercession and help.

It is good to reflect on the saints we have known. We all remember people who never made the headlines, but lived holy lives, loved Jesus, and blessed others with their kindness and generosity. I have known many such saints, and I often turn to them for encouragement and direction. In the lives of our own saints, we find courage and strength; we discover patterns that will guide us to the eternal happiness they now enjoy.

One category of saints we ought especially to remember are the little ones who die in miscarriages, at birth, or in the years of childhood. Parents of such children bear a heavy burden of grief, and their burden is often made heavier by uncertainties.

Some parents are sure that their child is in heaven because the child was baptized, but they wonder if their child will always be a helpless infant. When any human being dies, the limitations imposed by our physical body are left behind. Our physical body is transformed into a "spiritual body" (1 Corinthians 15:44). The elderly are no longer constrained by the burdens of age, nor are children confined by the restraints of infancy. One moment in the presence of God offers them more love and knowledge than could be gained in a lifetime on earth. Here they were dependent on their parents. In heaven they are "fully grown," able to help and guide their parents.

When infants die before Baptism, parents may wonder if they can go to heaven. Some Catholics have been taught that unbaptized infants go to Limbo, a place of eternal natural happiness, without the intimate closeness to God enjoyed by those in heaven. Limbo, however, is not official Catholic doctrine; it is a theological opinion not commonly accepted today. The *Catechism of the Catholic Church* (# 1261) states that we can entrust to the mercy of God all children who have died without Baptism, for God desires their salvation. We can be confident that Christ, who said, "It is not the will of your heavenly Father that one of these little ones be lost" (Matthew 18:14), waits for each little one with the same warm embrace he gave the children of his time. The liturgy of the Church, in its burial Mass for unbaptized infants, gives parents reason to hope in the boundless mercy and love of God.

Parents whose children die in miscarriages or in infancy should realize, then, that their children have gone before them into the presence of God. They should name those children, count them as members of the family, and pray to them often. One day the children they surrendered in sorrow will embrace them joyfully and welcome them to a home where there will be no more parting or pain.

Mary, Mother of Jesus and Our Mother

Among all the saints, Mary has a special place. She is the Mother of Jesus Christ. Because Jesus was miraculously conceived in Mary's womb by the power of the Holy Spirit, he is truly the Son of God and has no human father. Mary is the only person through whom Jesus Christ is related to us and to the rest of the human race!

She freely consented to be the mother of God's only Son. This was her highest privilege and accomplishment. But Mary's greatness shines forth in every action of her life. Soon after Christ was born, Mary was warned that she would be pierced by a sword, a sword of sorrow (Luke 2:35). Yet, she never backed down from her mission, even when it meant standing at the foot of the cross. She was a woman of faith and courage, of generosity and love.

No wonder the Bible states that "all ages" will call Mary blessed (Luke 1:48). No wonder she was greeted by the angel Gabriel with words that show God's esteem for her: "Hail, favored one! The Lord is with you" (Luke 1:28). She is the faithful "handmaid of the Lord" (Luke 1:38) who assents to God's will. She is "most blessed...among women" (Luke 1:42).

So Catholics honor Mary as Mother of God. We honor her also as our "blessed Mother." John's Gospel has Jesus address Mary as "woman" (2:4). This may well be a reference to the "woman" of Genesis, making Mary the "new Eve" and Mother of all the living. Jesus again addresses Mary as "woman" at the crucifixion: "When Jesus saw his mother and the disciple there whom he loved, he said to his mother, 'Woman, behold, your son.' Then he said to the disciple, 'Behold, your mother'" (John 19:26-27). The beloved disciple represents all believers, so at the very moment Christ redeemed humanity, offering us new life, he gave us his mother to nourish that life as she had nourished the life she had given him. Further, the Bible teaches that we are the Body of Christ (1 Corinthians 12:27). Our mystical, but real, identification with Jesus means that his mother is our mother too.

The Second Vatican Council explained the relationship of Mary to Christ, to the Church, and to us in the final chapter of its *Dogmatic Constitution on the Church*. It sums up our Catholic position on devotion to Mary. "Mary was involved in the mysteries of Christ. As the most holy Mother of God she was, after her Son, exalted by divine grace above all angels and men. Hence the Church appropriately honors her with special reverence" (SVC, *Church*, 66). The Council points out that true devotion to Mary differs from the unique worship paid to her Son, and always helps people to know, love, and serve Christ better.

We honor our earthly mothers, and we ought surely to honor our Mother in heaven. She once brought into our world its Savior, its Lord and God. She now longs to bring her Son into the hearts and lives of all of us, who are her children too.

Our Saints, Our Family

The saints are near, and in their presence we are in the presence of God, as the Bible testifies in a beautiful passage addressed to us and to all believers: "You have approached Mount Zion and the city of the living God, the heavenly Jerusalem, and countless angels in festal gathering, and the assembly of the firstborn enrolled in heaven, and God the judge of all, and the spirits of the just made perfect, and Jesus, the mediator of a new covenant" (Hebrews 12:22-24).

Hunter's parents have their special saint in heaven. We all have our special saints, our relatives and friends, who have gone before us. And, really, all the saints are our saints, for we are one family in Christ.

It is a privilege to be a member of the Catholic Church, which opens our hearts and minds to this family, to this communion of saints.

Questions for Discussion and Reflection

Who are your favorite saints? Why? Which saints do you pray to most often? What kinds of prayers do you say to them? What do you know about your patron saints? Do you think of Mary as your mother? Since Mary *is* your mother, what kind of feelings do you think she has for you?

The text speaks of those in heaven as "fully human." Sometimes people on earth think of those in heaven as not really human. But our heavenly existence is the perfection of human life. There we will be "fully human and fully alive," in the words of Saint Ignatius of Rome. What does it mean to be human? Is a baby in the womb human? Are we human? Are the saints human?

Can you describe some saints you have known? Do saints have to be perfect? Do you plan to be a saint someday? (What is the only alternative?)

Activities

Go through your family photo albums. Search for pictures of deceased friends and relatives. Think about their lives and their good qualities. Recall that those who have died in Christ are near you. Spend a few minutes visiting with them, thanking them for their good example, and asking them to help you follow Christ so that one day you may join them in heaven.

Relics are sacred objects venerated because of their association with saints. There are three classifications of relics. The first is the body of a saint, or part of the body, such as a portion of bone. The second is anything worn or used by the saint, such as a piece of clothing or a prayer book. The third includes articles which have been touched to a relic in the first classification.

Some people criticize Catholics for their use of relics. How would you answer someone who objects that the use of relics is superstitious and nonbiblical?

In forming your answer, reflect on the following considerations: Keeping such "relics" is a very ordinary human practice. Parents, for example, may keep a lock of hair from a child (first classification). They might have the child's baby shoes bronzed (second classification). They might treasure the first valentine ever given them by their child (third classification). Consider also that early Christians sometimes celebrated the Eucharist at the tombs of martyrs and that it has long been a custom to place relics of martyrs in consecrated altars. Finally, realize that it is incorrect to say that veneration and use of relics is nonscriptural. (See Acts 19:11-12.)

CHAPTER TWELVE
Catholic Theology

S ome stores and restaurants post a humorous sign near the cash register: "In God we trust. All others pay cash."

In God we Catholics trust. We believe in God, as we proclaim every Sunday in the Nicene Creed. But we also trust in others. We believe that God has revealed to people many supernatural truths which can be expressed in human language. These truths are, like so much else that is Catholic, a blend of the divine and the human; they are divine verities expressed in human words.

We believe that these truths have been entrusted to the Church, and that the Holy Spirit guides the Church as it studies and teaches them. One of the blessings of Catholicism is that we have "creeds" expressing our basic beliefs. The content of our faith is not purely subjective, left to the whim of individuals. It is objective, so that Catholics throughout the world, in every age, hold to the same essential truths.

Dogmas

The most essential truths of our faith are called dogmas. These are beliefs declared by the Church to have been revealed by God. They must be accepted by all who wish to be members of the Church. They include such truths as the Holy Trinity, the Incarnation, the Real Presence of Jesus in the Eucharist, Mary's Immaculate Conception, and the beliefs we profess in the Nicene Creed and the Apostles' Creed. All infallibly defined teachings of the Church fall into this category, as do those revealed truths which are taught by all the bishops in union with the pope as definitively to be held. (See Chapter Three.)

Official Teaching

Next in importance are instructions of the official teaching office of the Church: the pope and bishops, the successors of the apostles. Their teachings explain and elaborate upon the foundational truths found in the Bible and in sacred Tradition. Such teachings are presented in the encyclical (circular) letters and other statements of the popes, and in the documents of councils of bishops, like those of the Second Vatican Council. The Congregation for the Doctrine of the Faith, which assists the pope in matters concerning faith and morals, may, with the approval of the pope, issue doctrinal decrees containing official, noninfallible teachings for the whole Church.

Theology

The content of our faith has been further explained by theologians (those who study God and God's relation to us) like Saint Thomas Aquinas, Saint Alphonsus Liguori, and Saint Teresa of Avila. These saints and countless others have studied what we believe, how we should choose between right and wrong, and how we can develop our friendship with God. Their writings fill whole libraries and offer us a rich heritage of wisdom for our study and reflection.

There are many Catholic theologians teaching and writing throughout the world today. Their task is to take the authenic teaching of the Church and help make it understandable and relevant. If they are to accomplish this, however, they must remain faithful to the essential dogmas and official teaching office of the Church.

This requires faith, wisdom, courage, and prudence. The Second Vatican Council noted that, while the essential dogmas of the Church cannot be changed, our understanding of them can grow and develop. When theologians are attempting to explain doctrines like the divinity of Jesus Christ, they must express ancient truths in modern language, but without contradicting those ancient truths. Issues related to essential dogmas can be very sensitive, and it is not always easy to determine whether or not an opinion is in keeping with official Church teaching. For example, it is obvious that the divinity of Christ must be affirmed by any theologians who wish to present the teaching of the Catholic Church. But the related issue of when Jesus as man came to realize that he was God is not so obvious, and theologians have many opinions about this matter. Similarly, the fact that our universe was created by God is Catholic dogma, but questions about how God created it, how the teachings of the Bible on creation are to be integrated with the findings of science, and how humanity actually began are much debated.

The pope, bishops, and theologians may be restricted in their understanding of such issues by limitations in scientific knowledge or other fields of learning. Catholic leadership of the seventeenth century lacked the scientific knowledge to make correct judgments about the theories of Galileo. But the Church did not close off all inquiry into those theories, and subsequent study helped theologians and the teaching authority of the Church grow in understanding of the meaning of Scripture and its relationship to science.

In areas where issues have not been defined as dogma, there will be varying opinions among theologians. Theological investigations should be made with humility, openness to the truth, and willingness to submit to the teaching authority of the Church. The pope and bishops, the official teachers of the Church, have been promised the special guidance of the Holy Spirit. (See Luke 10:16; John 16:13; 2 Timothy 1:14.) The "Galileo incident" is well known precisely because it is one of the few incidents where official leaders of the Church erred in teaching religious matters! Therefore, even the noninfallible statements of the teaching office of the Church have a special authority that exists nowhere else, and theologians and all Catholics should attend to it.

Truth and Freedom

Some people object to the ideas of dogma and an official teaching authority, contending that dogma and authority stifle religious freedom. They argue that belief is primarily an act of the will and emotions, not of the intellect, and that belief is a matter between the individual and God. Their point of view is often expressed in words like "It doesn't matter what you believe, as long as you do believe."

This sounds very "democratic," but it is also a denial of the sacramental principle. It implies that objective truth is not a reality and that it cannot be expressed in human terms. It implies that the words of Christ do not have a basis in fact. Jesus Christ took bread and said, "This is my body." To say that it doesn't matter what we believe about the Eucharist is to say that the words of Christ have no objective meaning!

As we have already seen, words can have many meanings. How can we know what Christ actually meant? How can we reach the objective truth behind Jesus' words "This is my body" and behind all his other teachings?

The Catholic Church affirms that we must look to the Bible. On one occasion, Jesus asked the apostles what people were saying about him. They replied that some thought Jesus was John the Baptist, others Elijah, others Jeremiah or one of the prophets. Then Jesus inquired, "But who do you say that I am?" Peter responded, "You are the Messiah, the Son of the living God." Jesus then declared: "Blessed are you, Simon son of Jonah. For flesh and blood has not revealed this to you, but my heavenly Father. And so I say to you, you are Peter, and upon this rock I will build my church, and the gates of the netherworld shall not prevail against it. I will give you the keys to the kingdom of heaven. Whatever you bind on earth shall be bound in heaven; and whatever you loose on earth shall be loosed in heaven" (Matthew 16:15-19). This passage certainly shows the belief of the first Christians that Jesus intended to establish a Church, that Peter would have a special place in that Church, and that the powers of evil and death (the gates of the netherworld) would never overcome that Church. If the promise of Jesus means anything, it means that the Church under Peter's guidance cannot mislead in matters essential to the truth of Christ's gospel.

At the Last Supper, Jesus said to the apostles, "I have much more to tell you, but you cannot bear it now. But when he comes, the Spirit of truth, he will guide you to all truth" (John 16:12-13). The risen Lord told the apostles to make disciples of all nations, "teaching them to observe all that I have commanded you," and promised, "I am with you always, until the end of the age" (Matthew 28:20). Where will we find the truth of Christ? We will find it where the apostles and their successors are teaching in union with Peter and the successor of Peter, under the guidance of "the Spirit of truth." The Church is "the pillar and foundation of truth" (1 Timothy 3:15), and it is in the Church that the truth of Christ can be discovered.

Again, it may sound very "democratic" to say that all people should interpret the Bible any way they like, and that God reveals the truth directly to every person without any need for a teaching Church. It may sound democratic, but it is not what Christ said, and history shows that this attitude causes divisions, the proliferation of churches, and the mistaken notion that truth is what anyone wants it to be.

Christ came to bring us the truth. "Grace and truth came through Jesus Christ" (John 1:17). In fact, Jesus is "the way and the truth and the life" (John 14:6). He told Pilate, "For this I was born and for this I came into the world, to testify to the truth. Everyone who belongs to the truth listens to my voice" (John 18:37). Jesus taught many "truths" about God, about life, and about morality. Some of these truths were hard to accept, but Jesus did not back down from anything he had said. He did not tell people that they could believe what they wanted. He said that he was the living bread from heaven, and when people walked away from that truth, he did not call them back (John 6:22-71). He upheld the sanctity and permanence of marriage to people who believed in easy divorce (Mark 10:1-12). He proclaimed the reality of eternal life, and faced down those who thought the belief unsophisticated and naive (Mark 12:18-27). Yes, Christ came to bring us the truth, and he never deviated from the truth, even when it meant his death on the cross.

The early Church understood the critical importance of being faithful to the truth taught by Jesus. Paul is cited as saying to Timothy: "Take as your norm the sound words that you heard from me, in the faith and love that are in Christ Jesus. Guard this rich trust with the help of the holy Spirit that dwells within us" (2 Timothy 1:13-14). Obviously, the content of our faith was important to Paul! The First Letter of John berated false teachers who rejected Jesus as Messiah and Son of God (2:22), as well as those who denied the Incarnation (4:2). Such false teachers were "antichrists" (2:18-19).

God does not force anyone to accept the truth, but those who reject it do so at their own peril. True freedom does not mean foolish adherence to error. Picture someone driving on a dark mountain road on a rainy night. The driver stops and asks for directions, and learns that the road north leads home and the road south to a collapsed bridge. The driver is "free" to go south, but south leads to disaster. So, too, with the "directions" we receive from Christ. If we cling to the truth taught by Christ, we will find our way "home." If we decide to choose our own version of the "truth," we will end up in disaster.

In fact, just as the driver will be free to arrive home *only* if he takes the road north, so we will be free to find our human destiny *only* if we follow Christ. True freedom lies not in choosing anything that suits our fancy. True freedom lies in using our free will to follow Christ! "If you remain in my word," he told his followers, "you will truly be my disciples, and you will know the truth, and the truth will set you free" (John 8:31-32).

The idea that the Holy Spirit directs individuals to the truth without any need for the Church has been proven false by history. If the Holy Spirit actually guided people in their "private interpretation" of the Bible, they would all believe the same thing. Instead, those who have separated from the Catholic Church have splintered into thousands of different churches. The theory of private interpretation of the Bible simply does not hold up in the real world, but the Church has remained faithful to the truth of Christ for twenty centuries.

We who are merely human cannot completely understand or perfectly express all truth, all there is to know about God and the meaning of life. But Catholics believe that it is possible for us to distinguish between truth and error if we rely upon the Church. We believe that Christ guides the Church as we come to an ever clearer knowledge of the truth, as we study and express our "theology" under the leadership of the official teachers of the Church, the pope and the bishops.

Religious Freedom

One of the saddest events in all of human history occurred near the end of Jesus' public ministry. He had done his best to lead his people to the truth, but he had been rejected. As he approached Jerusalem shortly before his crucifixion, "he saw the city and wept over it, saying, 'If this day you only knew what makes for peace—but now it is hidden from your eyes. For the days are coming upon you when your enemies...will smash you to the ground and your children within you, and they will not leave one stone upon another within you because you did not recognize the time of your visitation'" (Luke 19:41-44). Because his people had rejected the truth of Christ, they were, Jesus knew, certain to accept the lies of those who wanted war against Rome. And such war was sure to bring doom upon his nation.

This incident teaches us much about Jesus' attitude toward religious freedom. He knew that his message was absolutely necessary for the temporal and eternal happiness of those who heard him. Acceptance of the truth was literally a matter of life and death for them. So Jesus did everything in his power to present the truth and to convince his hearers that they *must* accept his message—everything, that is, except the use of external force.

Jesus could have used his almighty power to coerce his listeners into following him. He could have struck down his enemies. He could have taken the power of speech from those who contradicted him. But he did not. Jesus, Word of God, gave the gift of freedom to human beings, and he would not take that gift away. He would finally give his life for the cause of truth, but even when his enemies taunted him as he hung on the cross, he would not use force against them.

This example of Jesus shaped the *Declaration on Religious Freedom* made by the Second Vatican Council. The Council set forth a number of principles that outline our Catholic belief about truth and human freedom. First, God has made known to us the way in which we are to serve God and find salvation and eternal life in Christ. Second, "this one true religion subsists in the catholic and apostolic Church, to which the Lord Jesus committed the duty of spreading it...." Third, all people "are bound to seek the truth, especially in what concerns God and His Church, and to embrace the truth they come to know, and to hold fast to it." Fourth, these obligations "exert their binding force" upon the human conscience, for "the truth cannot impose itself except by virtue of its own truth, as it makes its entrance into the mind at once quietly and with power." Fifth, human persons have a right to religious freedom, a right to be "immune from coercion on the part of individuals or of social groups and of any human power," so that no one is to be forced to act in a manner contrary to personal beliefs or prevented from acting in accordance with personal beliefs (SVC, *Religious Freedom,* 1–2).

The Catholic Church and Religious Freedom

The Catholic Church, therefore, acknowledges the existence of objective truth, the truth taught by Jesus Christ. The Church sees itself as divinely commissioned to preserve and teach that truth. All people are obliged, to the fullest extent possible, to search out that truth and to hold fast to it. But if people choose to reject Christ, then they must not be forced to do anything against their will. The judgment of their actions must be left up to God.

This is the official position of the Catholic Church, but it has not been universally accepted. From the time Jesus was crucified because he bore witness to the truth (John 8:40), thousands of Christians have been put to death because they were witnesses (martyrs) to the truth. Even today, some nations outlaw religion and punish those who choose to follow Christ. Regrettably, in past centuries, some Catholic leaders forced people to convert to the Church and persecuted those who refused to convert. Their intentions may have been good, but they violated the rights of those who were coerced, as the Second Vatican Council acknowledged. (See SVC, *Religious Freedom,* 12.)

It is the duty of the Catholic Church, then, to proclaim the truth of Christ. The Church must be firm, as Christ was firm, in proclaiming the truth. Jesus denounced those who refused to believe (Matthew 11:20-24). He expected his followers to have standards for membership in the Church, and he stated that those who violated them were to be excluded: "If he refuses to listen even to the Church, then treat him as you would a Gentile or a tax collector" (Matthew 18:17). The Church may not force people to believe in the teachings of Christ, but the Church has the obligation to protect the truth and to exclude from the Church those who would dilute the truth. Thus, the Church has a right to demand that those who claim to teach as Catholics must adhere faithfully to Catholic doctrine.

Religious truth, then, is an objective reality given us by Christ. It is found in the teaching of the Church, which is "the pillar and foundation of truth" (1 Timothy 3:15).

Catechism of the Catholic Church

In 1985 a meeting of bishops at Rome proposed that the teaching of the Catholic Church be presented in a catechism for the whole Church. Pope John Paul II immediately approved the idea, and a commission of cardinals, bishops, and scholars set to work on the project, which was completed late in 1992.

The *Catechism of the Catholic Church* is a summary of Catholic belief, presenting the doctrines, moral teachings, and spirituality of the Church based on Scripture and sacred Tradition. It is intended as a reference text especially for bishops and for those teaching Catholic doctrine and writing books of instruction on the Faith. The *Catechism of the Catholic Church* is of great significance because it presents the content of the Catholic faith in one volume, explaining in a clear way what the Church believes and teaches. As such, it is a sacramental sign, putting divine truths in human language and explaining to Catholics and all people of good will how those truths apply to our modern world.

In God We Trust

In God we Catholics trust. In others, especially the pope and bishops of the Church, we also trust, for they have been promised guidance by God's Holy Spirit. We trust that they, and theologians who are faithful to God's Holy Spirit, will lead us to a better understanding of eternal truth.

And because we see in God's truth the only way to real freedom and joy, we treasure God's wisdom and guidance offered by the Church to light our way through life. We echo the words of the psalmist: "How I love your teaching, Lord! I study it all day long. Your word is a lamp for my feet, a light for my path" (Psalm 119:97,105). The doctrines of the Church and the teachings which explain them are our theological heritage, part of the privilege of being Catholic.

Questions for Discussion and Reflection

How would you respond to the statements: "I would not want to belong to a Church with dogmas that dictate what a person must believe. It's impossible to be free in such a Church." Do creeds and laws always diminish freedom? Do the teachings of Jesus diminish freedom? Do traffic laws give us freedom to get where we want to go, or do they take away our freedom to travel? Who is more free, the person who knows the teachings of Christ and feels obliged to follow them or the person who has never heard the teachings of Christ?

Have you ever thought of the creeds of the Church and the official teachings of the Church as "Declarations of Independence"? Are they? Will you grow in freedom the more you know the truths of our Catholic faith, or will you lose your freedom by knowing those truths?

Activities

Write down at least ten of the truths you consider to be the most fundamental beliefs of the Catholic Church. Spend a few minutes reflecting on these truths. Ask God to strengthen your faith in these truths. Then reflect on the words of Jesus: "If you remain in my word, you will truly be my disciples, and you will know the truth, and the truth will set you free" (John 8:31-32).

CHAPTER THIRTEEN
Catholic Service

M other Teresa of Calcutta was one of the most respected women of the twentieth century. She was well known for her works of charity, but millions of Catholics through the centuries have understood, as she did, that Christ is present in all people, and in serving others we minister to Christ.

Catholics believe in the reality of life after death and look forward to an eternity of happiness with God in heaven. But we also believe that this life is good, and that it is our responsibility to cooperate with God in improving our world and in helping the poor and needy.

Anyone who looks at the world today will see enormous problems: war, racial strife, famine, disease, crime, disregard for the sacredness of human life, and an assortment of ills which may seem overwhelming. Some observe these evils and feel that a dark pessimism is the only possible response. Catholics are called upon by their faith, tradition, and history to recognize the goodness that still exists, to upbuild it, and to eradicate the evils that threaten it.

Our Catholic stance toward the world was expressed by the Second Vatican Council. "The joys and the hopes, the griefs and the anxieties" of people, especially of "those who are poor or in any way afflicted," are those of the Church. It is the duty of the Church to continue the work of Christ, who "entered this world to give witness to the truth, to rescue and not sit in judgment, to serve and not to be served" (SVC, *Pastoral Constitution on the Church in the Modern World,* 1,3). As Catholics, we are bound to build up the world and to attend to the welfare of other human beings. (See SVC, *Church Today,* 34.)

Service in the New Testament

The sacramental principle asserts that God is revealed to us in people, things, and events. Most significantly, God entered the world in the birth of Jesus Christ. Christ, in turn, is present for all time in his Body, the Church.

Further, we have Christ's own word that he is truly present in every human being, and that when we reach out to the poor and needy, we are actually reaching out to Christ himself. This will be made clear, Jesus states, at the Last Judgment. Christ will say to those on his right, "Come, you who are blessed by my Father. Inherit the kingdom prepared for you from the foundation of the world. For I was hungry and you gave me food, I was thirsty and you gave me drink, a stranger and you welcomed me, naked and you clothed me, ill and you cared for me, in prison and you visited me.... 'Amen, I say to you, whatever you did for one of these least brothers of mine, you did for me'" (Matthew 25:34-36,40). Every person in need is a sacramental sign of the Lord, Jesus Christ, and when we help the needy, we are helping Christ.

Motivated by Christ's teaching, the first Christians showed concern for not only the spiritual needs of others but for their physical necessities as well. They sold property and belongings, sharing the proceeds with the poor (Acts 2:45); they brought Christ's healing to the infirm (Acts 3:1-8; 5:15-16); they distributed food to the needy and ordained deacons to oversee this work of charity (Acts 6:1-7).

Saint Paul, before he became a Christian, learned that in persecuting believers he was actually persecuting Christ (Acts 9:1-5). He was converted by this awareness into one who helped Christ. He took up collections for the poor and urged believers to be generous in offering relief to the suffering (1 Corinthians 16:1-4; 2 Corinthians 8:1-24).

Other New Testament writings testify to the importance of works of charity. True religion means "to care for orphans and widows in their affliction..." (James 1:27). If we fail to give to the poor "the necessities of the body," our faith is dead (James 2:14-17). The First Letter of John exhorts: "If someone who has worldly means sees a brother in need and refuses him compassion, how can the love of God remain in him? Children, let us love not in word or speech but in deed and truth" (3:17-18).

Care for the Poor and Neglected

The Church's regard for service and works of charity is dramatically expressed in a well-known story told about Saint Martin of Tours, a fourth-century bishop. Before he was baptized, Martin was a Roman soldier. One day, seeing a poor beggar freezing in the cold, Martin divided his own military cloak and gave half to the beggar. That night in a dream he saw Christ wearing the cloak he had given to the beggar. This story may be legendary, but it has helped many generations of believers to realize that what we do for others we do for Christ.

Long before Martin of Tours, it was the practice of the Church to take up a collection for the needy at celebrations of the Eucharist. Saint Justin describes such collections at Rome around A.D. 150. The Christian community cared for widows, orphans, and other needy people, even when it was being persecuted by the Roman Empire. After Roman persecution ended in 313, Christians expanded their services to orphans, the abandoned, and others.

Such charitable work has continued to our own day. The Church devotes a great deal of attention to the poor and abandoned throughout the world. Many dioceses and parishes maintain food kitchens for the hungry and shelters for the homeless. Rectories and convents are "popular" stops for needy travelers, and most priests and religious offer food, gas, and other assistance. American Catholics are familiar with special collections for the poor, and Catholic organizations supported by such collections provide every kind of assistance, often in a way which helps people to overcome their poverty. The extent of aid given by American Catholics is immense. Catholic Charities, for example, was the largest nonprofit charitable organization in the United States in 1991, with a total income of $1.84 billion. (The American Red Cross stood at $1.46 billion and the Salvation Army at $1.28 billion.) American Catholics, and Catholics throughout the world, pool their resources and serve Christ in ways that go far beyond anything the apostles could have imagined!

Care for the Sick and Elderly

Christ worked miracles of healing, and many of his apostles did the same. But the Church realized that Christ heals most often, not by miracles, but by the ministry of doctors, nurses, and others who care for the sick. "When you are ill, delay not, but pray to God, who will heal you," advised the Old Testament, "Then give the doctor his place...for you need him too" (Sirach 38:9,12). The Church, heeding this counsel, has always believed in the power of prayer *and* in the efficacy of good medical care, and has had a long tradition of building and staffing hospitals.

In the early Church, medical care and attention were provided through Christian centers led by deacons. In cooperation with bishops and priests, the deacons not only supervised charitable gifts to the poor but also furnished hospices for travelers, hospitals, and homes for the aged. Some deacons rendered medical care, serving as doctors or nurses. Early in the fourth century, Emperor Constantine promoted hospital construction, and soon there were large hospitals under Church auspices throughout the Empire.

As Christianity spread, hospitals were built in and near monasteries, and many religious orders included the care of the sick as one of their ministries. In the Middle Ages, there were numerous organizations of lay Catholics dedicated to the care of the sick and elderly, and most such work was done under Church supervision. By the end of the fifteenth century, thousands of hospitals and hospices existed throughout Christendom, many of them built in the shape of a cross with an altar at the center for the celebration of Mass. At times of war and pestilence, the hospitals were stretched to their limits, but history abounds with examples of heroism, dedication, and sacrifice, as many religious and laypeople gave their lives in service of the sick and dying.

After Protestantism began in the sixteenth century, many hospitals formerly under the care of the Catholic Church were confiscated by secular authorities, but many others remained under the care of the Church. Today, rising costs and changing social conditions place strains on any organization offering medical attention, but the Church continues to operate hospitals and nursing homes throughout the United States and the world. Organizations like Catholic Relief Services provide medical attention and food in emergency situations anywhere on the globe. In an atmosphere where increasingly difficult moral decisions must be made about the care of people, especially the unborn and elderly, the Catholic Church proclaims the values of Jesus Christ to a world tempted to forget them.

Education

Christ came to teach us the truth about God, about ourselves, and about the nature and purpose of human existence. Jesus was regarded by his contemporaries as a "rabbi," a teacher (John 1:38), and many passages in the gospels present Christ as a teacher. Matthew's Gospel, for example, shows Jesus in the Sermon on the Mount as the new Moses. As Moses brought God's law to the Israelites on Mount Sinai, so Jesus brought the new law, God's ultimate revelation, to all people on the "Mount of the Beatitudes" (Matthew 5–7).

The early Christians lived in a world dominated by the pagan educational system of the Roman Empire. Wealthy children attended schools that taught Greek and Roman literature and poetry. However, Old Testament Wisdom books taught that "all wisdom comes from the LORD" (Sirach 1:1), and that children were to heed their "father's instruction" (Proverbs 4:1). Saint Paul urged parents to bring up their children "with the training and instruction of the Lord" (Ephesians 6:4). Consequently, while wealthy Christian children frequented the pagan schools, the education offered there was supplemented by home instruction on the basics of Christianity. All Christians, poor as well as rich, received guidance from the Church through the reading of Scripture and the preaching of the gospel. Some Christian teachers, like Clement and Origen of Alexandria in the second and third centuries, operated catechetical schools where pagan philosophy and science were studied in preparation for advanced studies in Christian theology.

By the fourth century, the Church had developed a well-designed procedure for the preparation of candidates seeking Baptism. The program, a pattern for today's Rite of Christian Initiation, often lasted several years and included instructions on the Creed, Christian morality, and worship. By this time also, monasteries had become centers of learning in the East, and they soon spread to the West. In the sixth century, Saint Benedict developed a rule for monastic life which set aside several hours a day for study. Until the invention of the printing press in the fifteenth century, monks and religious women copied by hand manuscripts of the Bible, of religious works, and of the pagan classics; they were responsible for the preservation of culture and education after the collapse of the Roman Empire. Schools supported by monasteries, cathedrals, and parishes trained clerics and laypeople.

The Middle Ages brought about a revival in education with the founding of great universities, often built under the sponsorship of dioceses and monasteries. Such universities promoted learning in philosophy and theology, as well as in law, medicine, science, and the liberal arts. Perhaps the greatest of teachers was Saint Thomas Aquinas, who wrote works of philosophy and theology that are still influential today. Religious orders like the Dominicans and Franciscans promoted education and vied with each other in the pursuit of learning.

The Protestant break from Catholicism in the sixteenth century brought about a reorganization of the educational systems throughout Europe and elsewhere. Even before this, a tendency to secularism had crept into the universities, lowering esteem for theology and corrupting many clerics with a rationalistic humanism. After the Council of Trent (1545-1563), the Catholic Church sought to renew confidence in its teaching authority by clarifying doctrine, correcting abuses, and setting up a seminary system for the education of the clergy. New religious orders, notably the Jesuits, arose to champion Catholicism and Catholic education. The Jesuit pattern for schooling involved training in Latin and Greek as a foundation for other studies, such as history, science, mathematics, religion, and the Bible. After this came university schooling in philosophy, theology, medicine, or law. This program served as an educational model for centuries.

After the voyage of Christopher Columbus to the New World, the Spanish and French brought Christianity to natives of America. Life in America was such a struggle for settlers and natives that there was little time for higher studies. A few schools were established by Catholic missionaries in areas under French and Spanish control during the seventeenth and eighteenth centuries. During the same period, many schools and some universities were started by Protestant denominations in the eastern English colonies of North America. Jesuits founded a few schools in the colonies during this time, but legal restrictions and prejudice against Catholics forced the closing of most such schools.

Shortly after the American Revolution, Catholics began to build parish grammar schools. Many were staffed by religious women. Saint Elizabeth Ann Seton started a school at Baltimore in 1808 and founded a religious order of sisters which opened numerous schools throughout the land. Many religious communities came from Europe and established parochial elementary schools. By the end of the nineteenth century, forty-five percent of the eight thousand parishes in the United States had elementary schools. Few grade school graduates went on to high school during this time, and only about one hundred fifty Catholic high schools had been established by the end of the nineteenth century.

The first Catholic university in America was founded at Georgetown in 1791, and the first seminary, Saint Mary's, began classes in Baltimore in that same year. Other colleges and universities followed, and by 1900 there were about as many Catholic colleges and universities as high schools.

Much of the impetus for building Catholic schools was provided by anti-Catholic prejudice in public schools. Public school children read from the *King James Bible* and used history books which denounced "popery." There was a great deal of bias against Catholicism outside the schools as well. During the first half of the nineteenth century, a movement known as Nativism emerged. Nativists published hate literature against Catholics and burned some Catholic churches, schools, and convents. In such a hostile environment, Catholic schools were necessary for the survival of the faith.

By the twentieth century, public schools had become nonsectarian, but their secularism was unacceptable to Catholic parents and religious leaders. Catholic schools continued to grow in number, and by the 1960s almost five million children attended more than ten thousand Catholic elementary schools. Over one million students attended twenty-five hundred Catholic high schools. Three hundred fifty thousand students attended two hundred fifty colleges and universities. Finally, almost fifty thousand seminarians attended more than four hundred houses of formation in philosophy and theology.

Since the 1960s, spiraling costs and reduced numbers of religious men and women have put pressures on the Catholic educational system. By 1991, the number of Catholic elementary schools had dropped to seventy-three hundred, with about one million nine hundred thousand students. There were approximately thirteen hundred high schools, with about six hundred thousand students. Two hundred thirty colleges served more than six hundred thousand students, both Catholic and non-Catholic. The number of seminaries dropped to two hundred fourteen, and the number of seminarians to sixty-two hundred.

These figures are still significant, and they illustrate the great service Catholic education provides to the United States as a whole and to the Church in particular. Catholic schools consistently produce graduates who rank higher on standardized achievement tests than do their public school counterparts. This is true, as many studies have shown, even when Catholic schools take in students from disadvantaged situations. Indeed, providing Catholic education for the poor has been one of the most effective ways the Church has had of helping the poor. (For evidence verifying these statements and those in the next two paragraphs, see *American Catholics Since the Council,* Andrew Greeley, Thomas More Press, pages 129-149).

Further, Catholic schools are free to present life as it really is— a gift of God which has eternal purpose. Many public schools in the United States have removed any mention of religion from education. Worse, they have denied religion any place in human life and replaced it with secular humanism, which allows no purpose or meaning in life beyond this world. The harm this does to children really cannot be measured, but recent sociological studies done by the National Opinion Research Center show that Catholic school graduates rank significantly higher than public school graduates in scales of hope, happiness, and meaning. This is not surprising, because we are made for God, and if God is eliminated from education (as in many public school systems), then life is denied any real meaning or purpose. Catholic schools stand as a signpost to all that God is the essential reality in human life and must be included in any truly human educational program.

Hopefully, American Catholics will appreciate the many accomplishments of Catholic education in the past and the need for Catholic education in the future. Real sacrifices are necessary if Catholic education is to grow stronger in the twenty-first century, but again, as National Opinion Research Center studies have shown, the Catholic educational system produces results well worth the sacrifices. Christ is our true teacher, and Catholic education gives Christ his rightful place.

Religious Instruction

In the earliest days of Christianity, the Church focused its educational efforts on presenting the truths of the faith to candidates for Baptism and to baptized believers. The Church has continued to offer instructions to candidates and to believers through the centuries.

Since the Second Vatican Council, the Church has established the Rite of Christian Initiation of Adults (RCIA) for those wishing to receive the sacraments. The RCIA, with its four stages of Inquiry, Catechumenate, Enlightenment-Purification, and Post-baptismal catechesis (Mystagogia), stresses formation in doctrine, liturgy, Church life, and service, and involves the larger Church community in welcoming, instructing, helping, and praying for the candidates.

When sixteenth century religious conflicts accented the need for religious education among all Catholics, the Church set up the Confraternity of Christian Doctrine (CCD). This organization promoted instruction in the Catholic faith for children, youth, and adults. It was expanded and strengthened by Pope Pius x early in the twentieth century, and CCD programs were mandated for every parish by Church law in 1917.

There has never been a time when Catholic schools have been available to all Catholics in the United States or elsewhere. Consequently, CCD has been important in supplementing secular education with religious doctrine. Most Catholic parishes have a CCD program, and many dedicated laypeople offer their talents and time to teach religion. In 1991, throughout the United States, CCD programs of various kinds reached thousands of adults, over seven hundred fifty thousand high school students and over three million two hundred thousand grade school students. All Catholics should cooperate to support CCD programs, since they bring the teaching of Christ to so many.

Social Action

"The Spirit of the Lord is upon me, because he has anointed me to bring glad tidings to the poor. He has sent me to proclaim liberty to captives and recovery of sight to the blind, to let the oppressed go free" (Luke 4:18). Jesus quoted these words from the prophet

Isaiah to identify himself as he began his ministry in Galilee. Christ loves all people and wants justice and peace for all. Many of his parables, such as the story of the Rich Man and Lazarus (Luke 16:19-31), demonstrate Christ's concern for the poor and lowly.

The Catholic Church sees itself as called to continue Christ's ministry of caring for the poor and oppressed. Justice has been a concern of the Church throughout history, but as modern means of communication and transportation have made the nations of the world more dependent on one another, the Church has emphasized social justice and social action even more.

Pope Leo XIII, in his 1891 encyclical, *On Capital and Labor (Rerum Novarum),* clearly stated the position of the Church demanding justice for everyone. All the popes since then have spoken on justice as a Catholic concern and have encouraged Catholics to help the poor and oppressed. The Second Vatican Council also addressed this concern: "Christians should collaborate willingly and wholeheartedly in establishing an international order involving genuine respect for all freedoms and amicable brotherhood....This objective is all the more pressing since the greater part of the world is still suffering from so much poverty that it is as if Christ Himself were crying out in these poor to beg the charity of the disciples" (SVC, *Church Today,* 88).

It is beyond the scope of this book to explore the many ways in which Catholics strive to bring social justice to the world. But "it is the duty of the whole People of God...to do their utmost to alleviate the sufferings of the modern age. As was the ancient custom in the Church, they should meet this obligation out of the substance of their goods, and not only out of what is superfluous" (SVC, *Church Today,* 88).

All Catholics can be a part of the Church's efforts to provide disaster relief and aid to the needy everywhere in the world. Our gifts to Church collections, joined to the gifts of millions of others, can save lives and ease suffering. We can in some way support the Church's efforts to defend the unborn, the most helpless of human beings, and other groups deprived of justice. We cannot be actively involved in every social cause, but we can choose at least one organization devoted to justice where we can carry on the work of Christ through our participation, prayer, and monetary gifts.

Our Ministry of Service

Throughout the world, we Catholics have built up a huge network of services designed to better the human condition. We strive to serve the poor and needy in every possible way. We operate hospitals, orphanages, homes for the elderly, and schools. We maintain the world's largest nongovernmental relief agencies. We pool our resources in annual collections like Catholic Relief Services and Peter's Pence, and are thereby able to help in situations where as solitary individuals we could do nothing.

Mother Teresa's accomplishments stand as an example of what we are all privileged as Catholics to strive for, making our world, God's world, a better place because we see Christ, and serve Christ, in everyone.

Questions for Discussion and Reflection

What, in your opinion, are the most important services rendered by the Catholic Church in the world today? In what ways are you reaching out to Christ in the poor and needy?

A recent magazine article reported that a little girl who was silently praying her rosary on a public school bus was made to put the rosary away. Do you think that "separation of church and state" requires such policies?

Activities

Find a quiet place and meditate on the judgment at the moment of your death. Reflect whether Christ will be able to say to you, "I was hungry, thirsty, sick, naked, imprisoned, lonely, elderly...and you cared for me." Examine your own situation, your "time, talents, and treasure," and consider how you can share them with others.

CHAPTER FOURTEEN
Our Catholic History

P icture the apostles on the day after Christ's crucifixion: eleven frightened men in hiding, waiting for an opportunity to flee from the authorities who had executed Jesus. No one could have imagined that these eleven would have a future outlasting that of the mighty Roman Empire which then ruled the world.

Their future is now our history. We who are Catholic look back on almost two thousand years of divine miracles and human endeavors, of successes and failures, of persecution and perseverance, an incredible story which continues with us!

Our History
and the Sacramental Principle

Our history, like all that is Catholic, shows that God's creation is good. It demonstrates that God loves people and shares life, love, and grace with us in every situation and circumstance. It exemplifies the sacramental principle, for our history is a sign of God's presence and grace.

Only by God's grace could the Catholic Church have performed the great deeds it has done. Only by God's grace could the Church have endured the hatred and persecution of its enemies. Only by God's grace could the Catholic Church have survived in spite of its own human weaknesses. Our history, in a very real sense, proves that God exists, for without God's providence and protection, we would not be here today.

God's Providence: Past, Present, and Future

That is the main lesson to be drawn from a survey of Catholic history. Even a brief review of the most significant events in our past shows that God is with us. Another benefit to be drawn from a review of our history is that it helps us put the present in perspective: the Church is experiencing difficulties and persecution today, but in the light of our past, they are to be expected. Finally, a study of our past gives hope for the future: we have every reason to trust that God, who has not allowed "the gates of the netherworld" (Matthew 16:18) to prevail against the Church, will continue to protect and preserve us.

The Church of the Apostles

Catholic Church history begins with the preaching of Peter and the apostles on the first Pentecost (Acts 2). The same men who had run away when Christ was crucified proclaimed him to be alive and the Messiah long-awaited by the Jews. The preaching of the apostles can only be explained by their real experience of the risen Lord. Their perseverance in spite of harsh persecution levied on them by the same authorities who had crucified Christ can be explained only by their experience of the Holy Spirit promised by Jesus (John 15:18-27).

Those first preachers converted thousands to Christ. Spreading out from Jerusalem, they established communities of believers in Palestine, Asia Minor, northern Africa, Greece, Italy, and Spain. Soon they came to the attention of Emperor Nero, a madman who launched a bloody persecution of the Church in 64, killing Peter, Paul, and many innocent men, women, and children. The persecution ended with Nero's suicide in 68.

The Post-Apostolic Church: Evangelization and Persecution

In 70, Jerusalem was destroyed by the Romans, and Christians clearly saw themselves as people of a "New Covenant" (Hebrews 10:9), no longer tied to the practices of Judaism. Missionaries traveled far and wide to preach the Good News of Jesus, and its promise of Christ's salvation for all people was well received in an age when paganism was losing its appeal. Christian communities sprang up everywhere. Believers met in private homes, forming "churches" ministered to by deacons, priests (elders, presbyters), and bishops (overseers). By the end of the first century, there were three hundred thousand to five hundred thousand Christians from India to western Europe.

Such a vast number of believers needed leadership if they were to see themselves as one Church. After the destruction of Jerusalem, such leadership came from cities like Antioch, Ephesus, Alexandria, and Rome. Of these, Rome became the most prominent. It was the center of the Mediterranean world. It was the city where Peter, first among the apostles, had been bishop and where Peter and Paul had died. By the end of the first century, Clement, bishop of Rome, was showing concern for other churches. During the second century, sacred writers were expressing the view that all the other churches must be one with the church of Rome in doctrine and policy.

But Roman civil government proved hostile to Christianity. The Roman Empire had a state cult that adored pagan gods and, at times, the emperor himself. Christians, unwilling to participate in such pagan worship, found themselves at odds with the state and were often accused of being disloyal. The emperor, Domitian (81-96), launched a general persecution of Christians late in his reign. After him, there was an official policy under which Christians were liable to arrest, confiscation of property, slavery, torture, and death. Some emperors did not actively pursue Christians, but others did, including Trajan (98-117), Marcus Aurelius (161-180), Decius (249-251), and especially Diocletian (284-305). Historians debate about how many Christians died during the Roman persecutions, but the numbers probably ran into the tens of thousands.

Edict of Milan: Religious Tolerance

In spite of persecution, Christianity continued to spread, and there were several million believers by the year 300. In 313, the Roman emperor, Constantine, issued the decree of Milan, granting religious tolerance to Christians. They were now free to worship and evangelize. The power of Christ's love had conquered the might of Rome, a miracle of history demonstrating God's providential care for the Church.

Constantine established his position in Rome, then eventually took control of the eastern part of the Empire, building a grand city, Constantinople, at the site of the old Byzantium. He promoted Christianity in the East and the West, and saw himself as its protector and advocate. This set up a new relationship between state and Church that allowed further expansion of Christianity. But it also opened a door to Church-state entanglements that would create new problems for the Church.

When the African priest Arius taught falsely that Jesus was not truly God, Constantine convoked the Council of Nicea in 325 to state the orthodox belief of the Church. Unfortunately, after Constantine's death in 337, his son Constantius interfered with the efforts of Catholic bishops to teach the Faith. Another general council at Constantinople in 381 further clarified the Church's belief about the Trinity and the Incarnation. The Nicene Creed, formulated during these controversies, is still prayed by Catholics at Mass.

During the fourth and fifth centuries, the Church developed its sacramental life. A program for catechumens was established which served as a model for modern RCIA programs. Other Church councils (notably Ephesus in 431 and Chalcedon in 451) defined Catholic doctrine. Famed teachers like Jerome (347-419) and Augustine (354-430) fostered study of the Bible and proclaimed the Faith.

The Church and the Collapse of Rome

In the fifth century, Rome began to collapse as barbarian tribes invaded her once secure boundaries. By this time, Roman civil authority had all but disappeared, and Pope Leo the Great (pope from 440 to 461) had to negotiate with barbarian invaders like Attila the Hun and Gaiseric the Vandal to save Rome from complete destruction.

But marauding tribes from central and eastern Europe continued to threaten civilization. Then in 496, the Frankish king, Clovis, converted to Christianity along with thousands of his people. He became a protector of the Church and began a relationship between France and Rome that would influence history for centuries. The Church became a civilizing force among Frankish and other peoples as they were gradually converted to Christ. Conflicts among the tribes and peoples of Europe continued, however, and few were safe from fire and sword.

Monastic communities, which had been in existence for several hundred years, mainly in the East and Africa, began to expand in Europe. After Saint Patrick's preaching in Ireland in the mid-fifth century, monasticism flourished in Ireland, and monks set out from there to evangelize the barbarian tribes of continental Europe. Saint Benedict (480-547) developed a rule of life for monks which would guide monastic life for centuries and turn monasteries into centers of spirituality and learning all over Europe.

The monastic movement provided one of the most outstanding leaders in the history of the Church: Gregory the Great, a monk who served as pope from 590 to 604. In the sixth century, Lombard tribes from Sweden and Germany had settled in northern Italy and threatened Rome. War and plague devastated the countryside, and Gregory cared for the sick and harbored refugees. Using revenues from the papal estates, properties which had gradually fallen under papal control, he fed the starving. Through negotiations, he managed to keep the Lombards at bay. He strengthened Church discipline, taught the Faith, and renewed worship. Like Leo the Great, Gregory ministered to both the physical and spiritual needs of his people.

Due in no small measure to the reforms instituted by Gregory, the Church in Europe expanded its missionary activities. During the 600s, whole peoples were converted in what is now England, Germany, the Netherlands, and elsewhere. Meantime, the eastern empire, with its capital at Constantinople, had been growing weaker. In the seventh century, the Church in the East came under the attack of Islam. Soon Islamic armies made inroads into Africa and Spain until they were turned back in 732 at Poitiers. Half a century later, Vikings began a series of raids lasting more than a hundred years against England, Ireland, France, and other lands.

The Holy Roman Empire

In 800 Charlemagne, a Frankish king who had united many of Europe's Christians under his rule, was crowned as Holy Roman Emperor. A powerful leader, he protected and promoted Christianity, but he also renewed Church-state ties, which would provide the occasion for later interference in Church matters by civil leaders.

The Holy Roman Empire, which included territory in Germany and Italy, would endure in some form or another until 1806.

Charlemagne died in 814, and unfortunately his successors did not match him in ability. His empire gradually degenerated into a feudal system where lords and dukes battled one another for dominance and where bishops and churches came under the influence of civil authorities. The years of chaos and confusion which followed are sometimes termed the Dark Ages.

Even during this time, monasteries survived as refuges for learning and the preservation of culture. In particular, a federation of monasteries centered at the abbey of Cluny (in the Rhone River Valley) early in the tenth century helped monks to maintain spiritual ideals and to serve the Church.

The Middle Ages

In the middle of the eleventh century, several strong popes brought about a reform which freed the Church of most of its entanglements with secular governments. Especially notable was Pope Gregory VII (1073-1085), who strengthened clerical discipline and set a pattern of strong administration and spiritual leadership for future popes to follow. The great tragedy of this era was the separation of the Eastern Christian churches from the Roman Church in 1054, a split which has lasted to our own day.

The eleventh century also saw the advent of the Crusades. Originally, these were meant to be military expeditions to free Constantinople and the Holy Land from Islamic domination. The first Crusade began in 1095 with a ragtag attack on Constantinople; a more organized army succeeded in liberating Jerusalem in 1099. But Jerusalem was recaptured by the Turks in 1187, and other expeditions by crusaders proved ineffective or disastrous.

The twelfth century saw the Church flourish in Europe. Monastic and religious life expanded under the guidance of such spiritual leaders as Saint Bernard of Clairvaux (1090-1153). Magnificent gothic cathedrals were built. Learning and the arts flourished, and universities were formed at cathedrals and monasteries.

In 1198, Innocent III was chosen pope. He ushered in the thirteenth century with vigorous programs to strengthen the Church. Innocent continued the reforms of earlier popes and presided over the Fourth Lateran Council (1215), which provided theological and disciplinary guidance to the Church for centuries. His influence lasted long after his death in 1216.

The Church expanded its influence on society through the development of great universities. Religious communities were founded by Saint Francis of Assisi (1182-1226), Saint Clare (1194-1253), and Saint Dominic (1171-1221). These and other communities of monks and nuns had a powerful influence on the spirituality of the Church. Many of their members, like Saint Thomas Aquinas (1225-1274), were renowned scholars as well.

After the Middle Ages: Decline

But by 1300 a decline had begun. In an effort to suppress heresy, the Church cooperated with civil powers to set up the Inquisition. The Inquisition at first had popular support, and it might be compared with the effort to root Communism out of America in the 1950s. Unfortunately, it lent itself to abuses as suspected heretics were harassed and tortured. Some were turned over to the civil authority to be executed.

A major crisis of the times was the move of the papal court to Avignon, France. Pope Clement v (1303-1316), a Frenchman, moved to Avignon in 1309, and his successors remained there until 1378. At that time, the cardinals divided into factions and elected two popes, thus initiating the situation known as the Western Schism. Two or three rivals claimed the papacy until the matter was settled by the election of Martin v in 1417.

There were many circumstances which contributed to the confusion of the period. The Black Death (1346-1350) wiped out half the population in many parts of Europe. War raged on between France and England and among many other countries as well. The havoc wreaked by such events and the disorder caused by the Avignon papacy and the Western Schism lowered the morale of the people of Europe and the prestige of the papacy. But even in these dark years the Church was not without its saints. Saint Catherine of Siena, Saint Bridget of Sweden, and Saint Frances of Rome are only three of the illustrious names of the period.

The fifteenth century brought the Renaissance, an era which saw a flowering of the arts and sciences, and a secularism that pervaded all of society. With the Renaissance came the most worldly popes in the history of the Church: Pius ii, Sixtus iv,

Innocent VIII, Alexander VI, and Julius II. These men patronized major achievements in art and architecture such as Saint Peter's Basilica and the Sistine Chapel, but they also meddled in politics and their worldliness scandalized the faithful.

Such corruption in the papacy and in other Church leaders, as well as interference by the secular authorities in ecclesiastical matters, made reform imperative. There were many saintly Catholics, both clergy and laity, who promoted renewal, but their pleas were not heeded.

Protestantism and the Council of Trent

In 1517, Martin Luther, a Catholic monk, posted his Ninety-Five Theses on a chapel door in Wittenburg, Germany, calling for an end to the abuses in the Church. At first, he wanted reform, not a new Church; but poor communications, stubbornness on the part of Luther and his Catholic counterparts, and interference by secular authorities led him to adopt positions which were irreconcilable with orthodox Catholic theology. He was followed in his break from the Church by Jean Calvin (Switzerland), John Knox (Scotland), Henry VIII (England), and many others. Secular rulers, seeing an opportunity to enrich themselves by seizing Church property, demanded that their people separate from Rome. Division followed division, and Christianity has since been split into many thousands of churches.

The Protestant break from the Catholic Church finally shocked Catholic leadership into serious efforts for reform. The Council of Trent (1545-1563) clarified Catholic belief, corrected abuses, and set up the seminary system for the education of clergy. A series of strong popes, beginning with the saintly Pius V (1566-1572), promoted a spiritual revival among the faithful and reformed the central governing authority of the Church. The accomplishments of Pius V included the promulgation of *The Roman Missal, Breviary,* and the *Catechism of the Council of Trent.*

Even before the Council of Trent, there were many reform movements within the Catholic Church. New religious orders arose. Saint Ignatius of Loyola established the Jesuits (1540), who were uniquely equipped by their discipline, spirituality, and learning to work for the upbuilding of the Church. Saint Angela Merici founded the Ursulines (1544), an order that would educate generations of Catholics. Many other saints and holy leaders worked tirelessly to strengthen the Church in faithfulness to Christ.

After Trent

After the Council of Trent, there were movements for reform within the older religious communities; Saint Teresa of Avila (1515-1582) and Saint John of the Cross (1542-1591) brought new life to the Carmelite Order and championed Church renewal in Spain and elsewhere. More new religious communities were established. In France, for example, Saint Vincent de Paul founded the Congregation of the Mission (1625) and, with Saint Louise de Marillac, established the Daughters of Charity (1633), a community which soon became the largest order of women in the Church. Many saints fostered spiritual growth in Europe and led missionary activities in the New World and elsewhere, bringing hundreds of thousands of new members into the Church.

During this period, Europe was troubled by wars and religious conflicts which continued into the seventeenth century. In England, Catholics were oppressed and ruthlessly persecuted. But reform continued throughout the Church, though Church-state quarrels in France and Germany made it more difficult. Another problem which had to be faced was Jansenism, a harsh spirituality that had originated in France in the seventeenth century. It advocated an unhealthy fear of God and discouraged frequent Communion.

This harshness was countered by saints like Margaret Mary Alacoque (1647-90), who fostered devotion to the Sacred Heart of Jesus. Saint John Baptist de La Salle (1651-1719) established the Christian Brothers, introduced new methods of teaching religion, and designed practical techniques to educate poor youngsters. Alphonsus Liguori (1696-1787), founder of the Redemptorist Order and one of the great moral theologians of the Church, emphasized the gentleness and compassion of Christ.

The eighteenth century saw the continuing evangelization of the Americas and other lands. Many holy spiritual leaders genuinely tried to improve the lot of native peoples as they shared the Good News of Christ, but they were often hindered by those interested only in exploiting newly discovered territories and in making profits from slavery.

At the end of the eighteenth century, the Church in France suffered a violent persecution. Leaders of the French Revolution tried to eliminate Christianity, sacking churches and murdering clergy and religious. Their agents attacked Rome, captured Pope Pius VI, and took him to France where he died a prisoner. The territories in central Italy (States of the Church) were annexed by France and were not returned to the papacy until 1815.

Problems generated by the Napoleonic wars caused further turmoil in Europe, and the Church spent much of the nineteenth century working out new relationships with rapidly changing governments. In 1870, the States of the Church were annexed by Italy, causing a breach between Italy and the papacy which lasted until 1929, when the Lateran Pacts granted Vatican City to the Church. This small area of one hundred eight acres under the rule of the pope is a state which functions to serve the spiritual needs of the Church and of humanity.

Throughout the nineteenth century, the principle of Church-state separation was much debated in ecclesiastical and secular circles. The Church experienced hostility from secular authorities and anti-Catholic groups. In the United States, for example, Catholics were persecuted by the Nativist party (sometimes called the Know-Nothings), and Catholics were denied many of their legitimate rights. Catholic immigrants to the United States were harassed, and the Church established schools, hospitals, and other organizations to care for them. In the United States and elsewhere, persecution seems to have strengthened the Church throughout history, and Catholicism grew steadily in numbers and influence as the twentieth century began.

The Twentieth Century

In the twentieth century, there has been a consistent movement in the leadership of the Catholic Church away from secular entanglements toward a more spiritual focus. Because the pope no longer has to govern secular territories, he is free to reach out to all people. The Vatican has become a center of diplomacy as the Church strives to promote peace and harmony among nations. The coming of so many Catholic immigrants to North and South America and the success of missionary activities all over the world have helped to make the Church more universal.

At the end of the twentieth century, there are about nine hundred million Catholics, almost one sixth of the world's population. The last one hundred years have seen a succession of remarkable popes who have led the Church through rapidly changing times to a point where the papacy is perhaps more respected and more influential than it has ever been. But these popes have also pointed out the ongoing need for reform if the Church is to be faithful to Christ. The Second Vatican Council, a gathering in Rome of all the Catholic bishops of the world in the 1960s, restated Catholic beliefs for the modern world and instituted many changes in worship and structure, encouraging Catholics to renew their efforts to follow Christ.

"The Gates of the Netherworld"

The twentieth century has presented many obstacles to Catholicism. The Church has had to deal with the devastation wrought by the two world wars and numerous other conflicts. Catholics have been violently persecuted by Communist governments in Europe and Asia and by anti-Catholic regimes in Mexico and elsewhere. Many thousands have been martyred. The Church has had to cope with prejudice from atheistic and secular humanism. In the United States and in many other countries, the media have been largely controlled by people hostile to religion in general and to Catholicism in particular. The constant barrage of antireligious and immoral messages spread by radio, television, movies, and the press has been a threat to the Good News proclaimed by Jesus Christ.

There are many challenges facing the Church today: materialism, atheism, secularism, disrespect for human life, the unstable condition of the international political scene, a shortage of vocations to the priesthood and religious life, just to name a few. And all its members are human, as fallible as were Peter and the apostles. Yet, our history should give us a sense of perspective about the present and the future. Jesus said to Peter, "You are Peter, and upon this rock I will build my church, and the gates of the netherworld shall not prevail against it" (Matthew 16:18). It's been almost two thousand years since Jesus said those words, and we ought to be ready to believe them by now!

Think for a moment of what it must have been like to be a Christian family imprisoned in the dungeons below the Colosseum during the Roman persecutions of the Church. Rats scurrying along the floor. Lions and tigers roaring nearby, raging with hunger, slamming against their cage doors. How could such a family have had hope, except the hope given by God? What chance would anyone have given the little band of Christians to survive the corrupt power of Rome?

Or think of the many priests, religious, and laypeople martyred during the French Revolution. If ever there was a time when the world went mad, it was then. Innocent people who had spent their lives serving others were marched to a cruel death by the worst kind of rabble. The enemies of the Church, the revolutionaries, were sure that the Church was finished.

In our own day, the Church was persecuted and assaulted by the guns and armies of Communism. Then almost overnight, the walls built on the sands of atheism came tumbling down, revealing that the walls built on the rock of Christ's promises still stood.

Through all the years the Church has existed, death has become life, tragedy has turned into triumph. The gates of the netherworld and the powers of hell have raged, and the Church has not only survived, but flourished. Surely this is a sacramental sign of God's presence in the Church!

Yesterday, Today, and Forever

Our past embraces the good, the bad, and the ordinary, and we who are Catholic accept it all as ours. We trace ourselves back to the Church of the apostles and see our bishops as the successors of the apostles. We have remained united to the successor of Peter, on whom Christ founded his Church.

Jesus chose twelve apostles. One of them betrayed him. But the scandal of Judas should not blind us to all that the other apostles accomplished. Eleven out of twelve is about a ninety-two percent success rate. By human standards, that's not bad! As we Catholics look back at our history, we've probably maintained that percentage with God's help. There have been Judases in the Church in every age, but there have been far more saints who now watch over us from heaven and encourage us to be faithful to the Catholic Church today.

So the Catholic Church has marched through the centuries as the Body of Christ down to the point where we are part of its mission. That is another great privilege of being Catholic. We are one in the Church. Our lives, our histories, are part of the life and history of the Catholic Church, the Body of Christ. And we move ahead into a future which gradually becomes our past, until future and past become "today forever" in the presence of the One we serve. For in heaven, "Jesus Christ is the same yesterday, today, and forever" (Hebrews 13:8).

Questions for Discussion and Reflection

If you could go back in time and live at any age in Church history, when would it be? Why? What era in Church history is the one you would least like to live in? Why? At what point in history do you think the Church has been most successful in following Christ? At what point in history do you think the Church reached its lowest point in terms of faithfulness? At what point do you think the Church has been most threatened by external forces? Is today a good time for the Church? Why or why not?

Activities

Review this chapter. For each century of the Church's existence, write down what you consider to be a high point and a low point. Then pray for a few minutes, thanking God for guiding the Church in our successes and bringing us through our failures. Make an act of trust in Christ, who has promised us that he will be with us all days until the end of time.

CHAPTER FIFTEEN
Our Catholic Way
of Growing Old

G rowing old is something we'll all do if we live long enough. So it might seem strange to speak of a "Catholic way of growing old."

But our Catholic view of life gives us a distinctive way of seeing old age. Our Catholic tradition offers special helps as the years of our life increase. Our Catholic Church brings us comfort, strength, and peace as we enter our last days on this earth. Our Catholic vision of death as birth to new life assures us that we shall live in an eternity that brings more, not less, of all that we hold dear.

Many people dread old age. The Old Testament book, Ecclesiastes, saw our last years as "evil days" (12:1-8). None of us looks forward to the limitations of old age or to the sickness and suffering that can precede death. But it is possible to entrust our last days to God. It is possible to reflect on the blessings God offers us through the Catholic Church and so to be freed from needless anxiety.

The Blessing of the Sacrament of Penance:
Pardon and Peace

Old age is a time when people know they will soon stand before the judgment seat of God. Some look back over their lives and worry about past failings. All are conscious of human frailty.

The sacrament of Penance allows the elderly to discuss their fears and faults, to hear Christ forgive their sins in the words spoken by the priest: "God, the Father of mercies, through the death and resurrection of his Son has reconciled the world to himself and sent the Holy Spirit among us for the forgiveness of sins. Through the ministry of the Church may God give you pardon and peace, and I absolve you from your sins in the name of the Father, and of the Son, and of the Holy Spirit."

Penance makes present to the elderly the mercy of God, the love of Jesus, and the peace of the Holy Spirit. It gives sacramental certainty that sins have been forgiven. Through this sacrament, the elderly find pardon and peace.

The Blessing of the Holy Eucharist: Union with Christ

I have often had the privilege of ministering Holy Communion to the elderly. I have always been touched by their devotion and their desire for union with Jesus, truly present in the Eucharist. This is so, I think, because Jesus more than fills the emptiness left by what they lose.

The elderly may have to leave their homes and possessions. They may lose their privacy and much of their independence. Their eyesight and hearing grow dim. Their limbs weaken. Friends die. But it is possible to count so much loss as gain, for it makes room for Christ. Saint Paul wrote: "For his [Christ's] sake I have accepted the loss of all things...that I may gain Christ and be found in him...depending on faith to know him and the power of his resurrection and [the] sharing of his sufferings by being conformed to his death" (Philippians 3:8-10). Each time the elderly receive Christ in Holy Communion, they are given the opportunity to fill their emptiness with Jesus Christ.

Union with Christ, realized in Holy Communion, also includes the union of our will with God's will. At Communion, we become one with Christ who endured agony in the Garden of Gethsemane. We receive from him the strength to conform our will to God's as we pray in his words, "My Father, if it is possible, let this cup pass from me; yet, not as I will, but as you will" (Matthew 26:39). With Christ in our hearts, we are empowered to give of ourselves until we become, like Christ on the cross, a sacrificial offering to the

Father. We thus obey Saint Paul's mandate to "offer your bodies as a living sacrifice, holy and pleasing to God, your spiritual worship" (Romans 12:1).

The Eucharist is for Catholics a sign that sickness and old age are not merely evils to be endured. They are unique opportunities for growth in holiness. Jesus said, "Whoever wishes to come after me must deny himself, take up his cross, and follow me" (Matthew 16:24). By bearing the crosses associated with old age, ordinary people become saints. And the Eucharist helps Catholics become saints by carrying their crosses in union with Christ, because it is a sacrament making Christ's death on the cross present today. "For as often as you eat this bread and drink the cup, you proclaim the death of the Lord until he comes" (1 Corinthians 11:26).

Marguerite, ninety years old and afflicted with diabetes, was told by her doctors that both her legs would have to be amputated. On the night before the surgery, her daughter-in-law Mary visited her and could not hold back tears as she entered the hospital room. Marguerite, in spite of what faced her the next day, looked gently into Mary's eyes and said, "Don't cry, dear, I'll get my legs back in heaven." Here was a woman who achieved holiness by joining her life and sufferings to the life and sufferings of Christ. Her words show that eucharistic union with Christ on earth is a sign and a foretaste of our union with Jesus in heaven, where he "will wipe every tear... and there shall be no more death or mourning, wailing or pain" (Revelation 21:4).

The Blessing of Catholic Prayer: Friendship with God

Sickness and old age can be special times of prayer. In our modern world, we are so busy and life is so hectic that we seldom pray as we should. When we are immobilized by traction in a hospital bed or by old age in a wheelchair, we have a unique opportunity to "get in touch with God," to pray for ourselves and others, to get ready for judgment and for eternal life.

Of course, all those who believe in God can pray. But we who are Catholic are blessed by our heritage and by sacred Tradition with methods of prayer that are especially suitable for old age. Our Mass and sacraments offer familiar patterns of prayer that help the elderly commune with God. The sight, sound, scent, touch, and taste which make up the signs of the sacraments can bring forth a response from people otherwise apparently lost in the tangled web of accumulated years and disabilities. I will never forget my Aunt Lena, almost one hundred years old, whispering the words, "My Lord and my God," as I elevated host and chalice after the consecration. Or a room of elderly people coming together in prayer as the Mass began with the Sign of the Cross.

The rosary is a prayer that has special meaning for many of the elderly. They can no longer see well enough to read from their favorite prayer books and they can't remember many of the prayers they memorized as children. But they can finger their beads and recite the Our Fathers and Hail Marys.

Anna was paralyzed by a stroke, and had control only of her right hand and arm. She lay in bed for seven years, praying the rosary. Only God knows how many people were opened to divine grace by the thousands of times she prayed her beads.

The Hail Mary itself is, of course, a beautiful prayer that offers assurance of our Blessed Mother's care and protection. We ask Mary, who stood close to her Son as he died on the cross, to be close to us: "Holy Mary, Mother of God, pray for us sinners, now and at the hour of our death."

The sacramentals of the Church help the elderly to pray. Crucifixes and medals give them a heavenly hand to hold. Statues on a nearby table, scapulars pinned to the bed, and holy pictures on the walls remind them of the saints and angels who watch over them and keep them company. Holy water refreshes them with the touch of God's grace and the assurance of eternal life given them—perhaps many years before—at Baptism.

In all their ways of praying, the elderly need to keep in mind that prayer is the most important ministry of the Church and the most powerful force on earth. "I feel so useless because I can't do anything" is a lament often heard in nursing homes. This, of course, is a cry of distress, and we should acknowledge the pain. But the elderly must be reminded that they can perform life's most significant work: prayer. Saint Therese of Lisieux is honored as the patron saint of missionaries, even though she never preached the gospel on foreign soil. But she prayed, even when terminally ill, for missionaries, and her prayers made their efforts more fruitful. Mary, in her appearances at Fatima, said that Russia would be converted, not through political activism or military might, but by prayer. Prayer changes lives and prayer can change the world. No one who prays should ever feel useless!

Those who understand the power of prayer find peace and joy. The same Marguerite who endured the amputation of both legs with such patience had to spend her last months in bed. When asked if time went by slowly for her, she responded, "Oh, no! The days are never long enough for all the prayers I want to say for my family and friends." Those who know the power of prayer find tranquillity and bring heaven down to earth.

The Blessing of the Anointing of the Sick: Healing and Salvation

The sacrament of the Anointing of the Sick is Christ's special gift to those who are seriously ill or burdened with the weakness of old age. The Church has always believed that through this sacrament Christ comes to the afflicted to "save" them, to "raise" them up, to forgive their sins (James 5:14-15).

Anointing of the Sick brings God's saving grace to the sick and elderly. The ritual for Anointing explains that this sacrament gives God's grace to the sick for the good of the whole person. The sick are encouraged to trust in God and are fortified against temptation and anxiety. Such spiritual benefits are always available through this sacrament.

The physical benefits of the sacrament vary. At times, Anointing brings noticeable, even miraculous, improvement in the physical condition of the sick. At times it expedites the medical procedures being administered to them. When this happens, Christ takes the sick by the hand and raises them up for a return to their everyday responsibilities, as he did the mother-in-law of Peter (Mark 1:31).

At other times, in God's providence, Anointing gives people peace and hope in the face of approaching death. Not long before my mother died, she became weak with pneumonia. I went to her hospital room and said, "Mom, I'm going to anoint you and give you Holy Communion." She smiled and whispered, "Good. Then I'll be all ready to fly away to heaven." Through Anointing, Christ does take the sick by the hand and raise them up to eternal life!

Christ is always present to forgive sins through this sacrament.

When a person is unable to receive the sacrament of Penance because of disabilities, Anointing of the Sick gives assurance of Christ's pardon.

The Catholic ritual for Anointing of the Sick points out another important effect. It helps the sick to bear suffering bravely and to conquer it. Some people must endure the crosses of suffering and old age for many years. They may wonder if they have been abandoned by God or even if they are being punished. The sacrament of Anointing can relieve them of such fears. The reasons for their suffering may still be unclear, but when they are anointed with the cross, they are reminded that the innocent Jesus endured unspeakable agony on his cross and is with them in their pain. They can say with Saint Paul: "I have been crucified with Christ; yet I live, no longer I, but Christ lives in me" (Galatians 2:19-20).

Through Anointing, the sick and elderly are encouraged to realize that suffering can be redemptive. The fact that they receive the sacrament as members of the Church from a minister of the Church assures them that they are part of the Body of Christ. This gives their sufferings the power to bring God's grace and love to others through the Church. Saint Paul wrote: "Now I rejoice in my sufferings for your sake, and in my flesh I am filling up what is lacking in the afflictions of Christ on behalf of his body, which is the church" (Colossians 1:24). Christ's sufferings and death were sufficient to redeem humankind, but Christ needs the suffering members of his Body to channel his redemptive love to the world. All they need do is picture themselves in their sufferings next to Christ on his cross, and join their sufferings to his for the sake of the Church and the world.

When the sick freely offer up their suffering on behalf of others, it calls down the love and mercy of God. Christ allows the sick to do more than endure suffering. He makes it possible for them to turn suffering into prayer on behalf of his Body, the Church.

The Blessing of the Funeral Liturgy: To Live Fully and Forever

Phil was a highly respected businessman and a good friend to many. He died after a long illness, and the church was crowded for his funeral. After the Mass, a young woman approached the celebrant and said with a smile, "I'm not Catholic, but when I die I want to be buried in a Catholic funeral service!"

Catholic funeral services are different. We pray for those who have died. This is a comforting practice, for it means that when we attend the funeral of a loved one or stand at the grave, we are not helpless onlookers. By God's grace, we can assist the faithful departed by our prayers.

Some people may die with attachments to lesser sins, or without having done sufficient penance for their sins. Such persons would not be cut off forever from God, but would need further "purification" (traditionally called purgatory) to stand in God's presence where "nothing unclean will enter" (Revelation 21:27). The Catholic Church believes that those who have died are not beyond our reach. They can be helped by our prayers.

This belief goes back to Old Testament times. About 165 B.C. some Jewish soldiers fighting in a war for independence under the great leader, Judas Maccabeus, were slain in battle. They were found to be wearing pagan amulets, a practice forbidden by Jewish law. The other Jewish soldiers prayed for them, and Judas sent money to Jerusalem to offer an expiatory sacrifice for them. The Bible comments that this was "holy and pious," and affirms that "he made atonement for the dead that they might be freed from this sin" (2 Maccabees 12:46). Inspired by this passage, Catholics have always prayed for their beloved dead, as inscriptions in the Roman catacombs and early writings of Church leaders show.

In the sixteenth century, Protestant leaders repudiated the idea of purgatory. In response, the Council of Trent declared as doctrine the existence of purgatory and the possibility of helping the souls there by our prayers. But the exact nature of purgatory is unclear. Some have believed that the purification of purgatory is brought about through fire, but this cannot be physical fire, since those in purgatory do not have physical bodies. The "fire" of purgatory is the fire of God's love. "For our God is a consuming fire" (Hebrews 12:29), and just as fire burns away impurities when gold is refined, so God's love will "burn away" the imperfections that could keep us from being perfectly open to the presence, love, and joy of God.

The funeral Mass reminds us of another reality as we ask for the intercession of the saints. This asking expresses our belief that those in heaven care for us and help us by their prayers. They see

God as God really is (1 John 3:2) and by the wisdom and love of God are more aware of us on earth than we are of one another. They have "a spiritual body" (1 Corinthians 15:44) whose abilities surpass ours more than an adult's abilities surpass those of a baby in the womb.

I have often been asked by people, many of them not Catholic, if their loved ones who have died are aware of what happens here on earth. Are grandparents in heaven, for example, able to celebrate a grandchild's Baptism or birthday? I feel blessed to share with them the certainty of our Catholic doctrine of the communion of saints, which affirms that friends in heaven know us and pray for us. We can talk with those who have died in Christ's love, for they watch over us, hear us when we turn to them, and assist us by their prayers.

It can be a great source of consolation and strength to the elderly to know that as the years go by and our friends on earth grow fewer, our friends in heaven increase. One elderly gentleman said, "Before my wife died, we used to go dancing a lot. We can't do that anymore, but now we talk."

It should also be a source of consolation to know that, when our life on earth ends and we are privileged to join our friends in heaven, we will not be deprived of our friends on earth. We will be close to them. We will be able to assist them by our prayers. We will one day welcome them into the joys of heaven.

Catholic Attitudes Toward Old Age and Death

It is likely that most of us will experience old age. We will all certainly die. Our attitudes toward old age and death are, therefore, very important to our happiness and well-being. Reflecting on the blessings God offers us through the Catholic Church can help us develop attitudes that will strengthen us in faith, hope, love, and peace of soul.

What ought to be our attitudes toward suffering? First of all, we should avoid complaining and self-pity. These do no good, but only serve to make us and others more miserable. Then we should try to accept unavoidable suffering with humor and good grace, uniting it to the suffering of Christ for the salvation of others. Some people even learn to joke about the inconveniences of old age. One old gentleman, when asked how he kept his teeth from chattering in the cold weather, replied, "It's easy. I just keep them in the bathroom cabinet."

We would do well also to avoid statements like "I hope I'll never have to go to a nursing home" or "I'd rather die than spend my last years in a nursing home." Such statements only develop attitudes guaranteed to make us unhappy. We will do far better to say things like "I leave my last years in the Lord's hands," and then to offer a little prayer doing just that.

When we find ourself worrying about death, wondering how we shall be able to endure something so frightening and so unknown, we must remember that death seems fearful now because God cannot give us the grace to die now when we are not dying! When the time comes for us to die, God will give us the grace, and it will be sufficient. In my more than twenty-five years as a priest, I have never seen a faithful Catholic die a "bad" death.

Mary was told by her doctor that she had inoperable cancer. She asked to talk to a priest, and told me how fearful she was of death. I shared with her the fact that God wasn't giving her the grace to die just then, because it wasn't her time to die. She was a woman of faith, and returned to her family and job. One of her hopes was to dance at her daughter's wedding, and she did, more than two years after the diagnosis of cancer. Some months after the wedding, she lay on her deathbed, peaceful and ready to die, confident that she would soon be fully alive in heaven. It was now her time to go and be with the Lord, and the Lord was there to give her the grace to accept death, to take her by the hand and lead her to eternal life.

I have noticed that as people get closer to death, they become more certain that they are moving toward God. I have always considered this a proof of God's existence. If there were no God, dying people would be moving toward nothing, and they would know it. But because there is a God, death brings them nearer to God, and this fact should make us confident that death will bring us to God.

God will give us the grace to die when our time comes to die. Jesus will be at death's door to welcome us to eternal life. These are the graces of a happy death, and if we want a happy death, we should pray for it.

John was dying in a veterans' hospital after a long bout with lung cancer. He had borne his illness for years without complaint, but now he seemed fearful. I asked him why. "I'm not afraid of dying," he said, "but I'm afraid of the pain." I inquired, "How would you like to die?" "In my sleep," he replied. So we prayed for that grace from God, and the next morning John died peacefully in his sleep, with his daughter at his bedside.

Finally, we can overcome our fear of death if we consider that it is really birth to eternal life. Babies experience uncertainty and pain when they die to life in the womb in order to be born into this life. We will experience some uncertainty and pain as we go through death, but when we realize that it is birth to new life, we can say with Saint Paul: "I consider that the sufferings of this present time are as nothing compared with the glory to be revealed for us" (Romans 8:18).

Growing Old to Be Forever Young

The blessings of the sacraments of Penance, Eucharist, and Anointing of the Sick, of Catholic prayer and the Catholic funeral liturgy, provide absolute assurance that Christ is with us in old age and through death itself. They are gifts from Christ to us, shared with us through his Body, the Church. They assure us that Jesus will help us bear our crosses and that death will be a moment of birth to new life where old age will be only a pleasant memory and we shall be forever young.

There is a Catholic way of growing old. May God bless us with the realization that it is not something to be dreaded, but a privilege which will usher us into the presence of our friends, of angels and saints, of Jesus and the Father and the Spirit.

Questions for Discussion and Reflection

Sometimes we hear people say, "It doesn't matter what church you belong to or what you believe, as long as you believe." After studying what Catholics believe about old age, do you think that it really doesn't matter what we believe? Does it matter whether we believe that Christ is really present to forgive our sins in the sacrament of Penance, that Christ is really present in Holy Communion, that Christ is there to take us by the hand in the Anointing of the Sick? Do you think it matters if we believe that while our friends on earth decrease, our friends in heaven increase (especially since this is true)? Does it matter whether or not we believe that we can talk with the saints and with our loved ones who have died (especially since this is a fact)? Does it matter whether we believe that after death we shall be in touch with our loved ones on earth (and we will)? Does it matter whether we believe in the truth or in partial truth or in error?

Are you afraid of death? How would you like to die? Do you pray often for a happy death?

Activities

You may want to memorize and pray the following traditional Catholic petition for a happy death: "Jesus, Mary, and Joseph, I give you my heart and my soul. Jesus, Mary, and Joseph, assist me in my last moments. Jesus, Mary, and Joseph, may I breathe forth my soul in peace with you."

CHAPTER SIXTEEN
Catholic Evangelization

> Wherever the Catholic sun does shine,
> There's music, laughter, and good red wine.
> At least I've always found it so.
> *Benedicamus Domino!*
>> Adapted from Hilaire Belloc's
>> *The Path to Rome*

"Benedicamus Domino!" "Let us bless the Lord!" We Catholics have a heritage of belief in the Incarnation of Jesus that should make us want to bless and praise the Lord. We believe that Jesus has hallowed all of creation, that he is present in our world and in people, in "music, laughter, and good red wine." We express our belief in the way we treasure the Church, the Bible and sacred Tradition, the sacraments and the sacramentals, prayer and the communion of saints, theology and service, Church history and our personal history.

Acknowledging the greatness of our Catholic Church should not make us look down on other churches. We should respect the sincere beliefs of others and see the genuine goodness in many holy people of every creed.

But we should also, because we are Catholic, learn all we can about our faith. We should evangelize, which means that we should witness to our faith and share it with others. "Always be ready to give an explanation to anyone who asks you for a reason for your hope" (1 Peter 3:15).

"An Explanation...a Reason"

"Always be ready to give an explanation to anyone who asks you for a reason for your hope." We who are Catholic have reasons for everything we hope in and believe. It is crucial, then, for us to really know our faith and to understand those reasons. Hopefully, this book will help us grow in knowledge and understanding. Other books explaining Church teachings may be found in the Bibliography.

Catholics who return to the Church after some time away often remark, "If I had known the teachings of the Church as I do now, I would never have left." Many people drift away from the Church because they are not sufficiently committed to its truths, and they are not committed because they do not really know them. Many others leave because of attacks against Catholicism: "Catholics worship statues"; "Catholics aren't allowed to read the Bible." Such biased assaults are patently untrue, but Catholics who do not understand their faith thoroughly may be misled by them to leave the Church.

Many Catholics today have excellent educations in secular fields. They may have college degrees or have done postgraduate work in science, literature, law, or many other areas. But their education in religion stopped at the grade school or high school level. They have an adult's knowledge of many things, but a child's awareness of their religion. No wonder some of them feel that religion is for children. No wonder some of them abandon their faith when they are challenged by calumnies against Catholicism.

So the first task of evangelism is to evangelize ourselves! The more we know about the Bible and Church teachings, the more we will be confirmed in the truth. The more we are confirmed in the truth, the more we are encouraged to live our beliefs, to pray, to be active members of Christ's Body, the Church, to be ready to give an explanation to all who ask.

Most often, the "explanation" behind our Catholic beliefs, traditions, and hope is the Incarnation of Jesus Christ. Because Christ entered this world and became truly human, material things and people reflect the presence of God. *Why do Catholics say the bread and wine become Christ?* "Because we believe that Jesus blessed creation by becoming human and now uses things to bless us." *Why do Catholics honor the saints?* "Because we believe that people are good, and that the saints will bring us closer to Jesus." *Why do Catholics use holy water and rosaries?* "Because we believe that the good things of creation put us in touch with our Creator."

The Incarnation of Jesus Christ is the center of human history. Through the Incarnation, God entered into our world and established a bond between God and us that can never be broken. Through the Incarnation, all created things were touched with the spark of divinity and began to radiate the Good News that God is with us. The sacramental principle expresses this reality, and we who are Catholic are privileged to believe in it and share it with others.

"Always Be Ready to Give...
To Anyone Who Asks"

With these words, the First Letter of Peter encourages believers to be ready to explain their faith to anyone who asks about it, to be ready to evangelize. However, many Catholics today feel uneasy about evangelizing. They consider it to be the duty of priests and religious, but not of laypeople. Some fear that they are not sufficiently qualified to talk about the faith. Others don't want to be "pushy" about their beliefs.

The First Letter of Peter, however, did not restrict its advice to ordained ministers. All baptized believers, as Pope John Paul II noted in his 1991 encyclical, *On the Permanent Validity of the Church's Missionary Mandate (Redemptoris Missio)*, are responsible for spreading the faith. To be sufficiently qualified to evangelize, people need not be professionally trained theologians; they need only to be willing to study their faith so that they really understand it. It is not necessary to be "pushy." Catholics respect the beliefs of others, and it is not our style to interrupt travelers at airports or to knock on doors to argue about religion. But Catholics must recognize that many people are searching for the truth and would welcome the opportunity to ask questions if they knew someone would be interested in answering them. How will they know this? Usually, through good example given by Catholics who live their faith and who seem friendly and approachable.

In more than twenty-five years as a priest, I have found that most people who have come to instruction classes or RCIA programs were drawn there by the good example of Catholic friends or neighbors. "Frank and Carol have something we are looking for," prospective converts might say. "They show so much love to each other, and their life has meaning. They really live their faith, and we want to be like them."

Note that such people are really saying that their Catholic friends have been a "sacramental sign" to them of Christ's presence and grace. Their friends are Christ to them by the kind of lives they lead. Love, honesty, integrity, generosity, concern for others, and respect for the lowly are qualities that make people "shine like lights in the world" (Philippians 2:15) and attract others to our faith. Usually, Catholics who evangelize by good example are proud of their faith and show it in little ways. They are not ashamed to make the Sign of the Cross before meals in restaurants or to wear ashes on Ash Wednesday. When visiting a sick friend in the hospital, they readily ask, "Would you like me to say a prayer with you?" They have symbols of the faith like crucifixes, statues, and a Bible in their homes, and even at their office or workplace. In these and many other ways, such Catholics let the world know: "I believe in Jesus Christ, and I am willing to give the reasons for my belief if you are interested."

We Are the Church

If the Church is to evangelize the world, then all Catholics must take responsibility for evangelizing. Sometimes Catholics think of the Church in terms of the pope, bishops, and clergy. They see that the Church ought to be doing something in a certain area, and then wonder why the Church is *not* doing it. They fail to realize that *they* are the Church, and something is not being done because they are not doing it!

Some time ago I heard that a young Catholic friend of mine (we'll call him Jim) had moved to a large city and joined a "nondenominational" Christian church. Back home on vacation, Jim explained that he could not find a "young-adult" group at the Catholic Church he was attending. He heard that a certain Christian church had such a group and so he investigated. There he met several other young men, former Catholics like himself. They were all frustrated because no Catholic churches in their town had a young-adult group. Soon Jim joined them in changing his church membership.

I asked Jim if he realized that he and his friends *were* the Catholic Church. I asked if he had considered whether God might have been inviting him and his friends to take responsibility for forming a young-adult group. If they had done so, they would have increased their appreciation of their Catholic faith and would have evangelized many other young adults in their city. The real problem was not that the Catholic Church was doing nothing for young adults. The problem was, sadly, that these young adults were not able to take responsibility for *being* the Catholic Church.

In contrast to Jim's response was the action taken by another young friend in a similar situation. Jenni enrolled at a small private college several hundred miles from her hometown. As a student, she attended a Catholic church near her college campus. The singing at Sunday Mass was poor because there was no song leader. Jenni approached the pastor and asked if she could help. The pastor was happy to say yes, and soon Jenni was leading the hymns at Mass. She made friends with a number of the parishioners, who were delighted by her talent and enthusiasm.

Then Jenni noticed that there was no Catholic student group at her college. She made friends with Catholics on campus and did some "homework" looking into successful Catholic student groups at other colleges. By her senior year, Jenni had started a Catholic student organization which met regularly to discuss the faith, to pray, and to enjoy social activities. They reached out to the high school youth group at the local parish and did apostolic work in their college town. As Jenni and the other students in their Catholic group graduated, they brought their experience and their ability to work with youth to many parts of the country.

Both Jim and Jenni were faced with situations where the "Church was doing nothing for young adults." Their circumstances were similar, their responses different. Jenni realized that she was the Church, and that Jesus Christ was asking her to evangelize, to be a sacramental sign of his presence at her college and parish. She said yes to Jesus, and through her, Jesus has touched many lives and hearts. The more all Catholics, young and old, respond to Christ's call as Jenni did, the more the Church will "make disciples of all nations" (Matthew 28:19).

The Domestic Church

The place where evangelization ought to begin is the home. As the Second Vatican Council pointed out, parents are the "first preachers of the faith to their children," and the family is the "domestic Church" (SVC, *Church*, 11). Parents, then, must share their Catholic beliefs and traditions with their children. Every Catholic family ought to be a "little Church," where children first learn about Jesus and his teachings, where they pray and serve and share.

In this domestic evangelization, Catholic traditions, prayers, and sacramentals can be helpful, because children relate easily to things they can see, taste, smell, touch, and hear. Parents of infants can make the Sign of the Cross on their children's foreheads and bless them with holy water from the day of birth. Blessing prayers said by parents over children are powerful expressions of parental love and divine care. Traditional Catholic prayers said by parents with their children join members of the family to one another and to God.

Statues and sacred images in rooms throughout the house remind children of the saints who watch over them. A crib scene reaches out to a child's sense of wonder and reminds all of the real meaning of Christmas. Advent wreaths, blessed palms, and blessed candles call liturgical observances to mind. A guardian angel "night-light" provides a comforting sense of security to a small child afraid of the dark. Gift giving at birthdays and Christmas can take on a spiritual dimension when parents present a Miraculous Medal along with a new shirt, a children's Bible with the toys, a statue of Mary with a new game.

It's never too early (or too late) to start. I've known parents who began evangelizing their child even before birth by playing religious music in the home during the months of pregnancy. The parents remarked that their child, shortly after birth, would smile or become active when they sang a melody that had been played often during the pregnancy! And it is good to note that parents cannot help but teach children something about God. If God is ignored in the home, children are thereby taught that God is unimportant. If God is emphasized, children are taught that God is God!

So parents should evangelize children, but children also teach adults, as when little ones fold their hands before a meal, reminding their parents of the grace they forgot to say. Or when children tell their parents the words they hear from Jesus and Mary in response to their prayers. Or when children touch the hearts of the parents by their innocence and simplicity.

Anti-Catholicism and Evangelization

In the first centuries of Christianity, believers were thrown to the lions in the Colosseum. Throughout history, Catholics have been maligned and persecuted. Even in the United States, a country whose Constitution provides the right to freedom of worship, Catholics have had to cope with persecution, prejudice, and hatred.

Perhaps the most blatant example of anti-Catholicism in United States history was the Nativist movement in the first half of the nineteenth century. Nativists were native-born Protestants who wanted to keep Catholic immigrants out of the country. Anti-Catholicism was taught in public schools. Books, periodicals, and newspapers poured out a flood of lies and distortions against Catholics, inflaming mobs that attacked churches, convents, rectories, and schools. In 1844, three Catholic churches and numerous other buildings were burned and thirteen people were killed in Philadelphia. Violence spread to other cities.

A political party, the American party, was formed. Its members always claimed to "know nothing" about its activities, and so it came to be called the Know-Nothing party. The party won several state legislatures and elected more than fifty members to the United States Congress. Wherever the party flourished, anti-Catholic riots and church burnings were common. The coming of the Civil War broke up the Know-Nothings, and violence decreased, but anti-Catholicism endured in many forms.

Throughout the nineteenth century and into the twentieth, anti-Catholics continued to print hate-materials against the Church. Such newspapers as the *Menace*, started in Aurora, Missouri, in 1911, produced fabricated articles which portrayed Catholics as sinister agents who plotted the overthrow of the United States and engaged in the worst kinds of orgies. The paper eventually reached a circulation of over a million and a half before it was forced out of existence by lawsuits in the 1930s. The nineteenth century also saw a great deal of anti-Catholicism and mob violence perpetrated by the Ku Klux Klan.

Well into the twentieth century, Catholics could not be elected to political positions in many parts of the United States, and no Catholic was elected president until John Kennedy took office in 1960. Publishers like Jack Chick rival the old *Menace* in turning out lies against Catholics, lies which are accepted with astonishing credulity by large numbers of people. Catholicism is still denounced from many pulpits throughout the country. A popular television evangelist proclaimed on TV and in print that all Catholics will be condemned to hell unless they leave the Church, a threat of condemnation frequently seen in hate-literature against Catholics.

Recent studies have shown that there is a pervasive bias against Catholicism in the media. Dr. Robert Lichter, director of the Center for Media and Public Affairs in Washington, D.C., did a careful survey of media attitudes toward Catholics. It showed that in almost all issues, the media stacked its reports against official Catholic positions and consistently spoke of the Church's authority in terms of oppression (*Columbia*, March 1991). Media biases against the Church have been noted in such magazines as *U.S. News and World Report,* which observed that no other group in our country is treated with such hatred and prejudice as the Catholic Church (April 1, 1991). An article in the November 1991 *Catholic Digest* noted that there is prejudice against Catholics even in the world of computer bulletin boards. A Catholic who observed frequent Catholic "bashing" on a fundamentalist bulletin board tried to respond with the Catholic position. He was informed that he had lost his bulletin board privileges because he "divided the Body of Christ."

In my ministry as a priest, I have frequently heard reports of Catholics being attacked by other Christians for their beliefs. Thankfully, most Christians treat Catholics and other denominations with respect, but there are some who seem to make a religion of denouncing Catholicism. We are accused of not being Christian. We are censured for worshiping statues. We are mocked because of our pro-life stance.

Why is there so much anti-Catholicism? Why so much hatred against the Catholic Church not only in the secular media but even in some church pulpits? The answer is simple. Jesus said, "If the world hates you, realize that it hated me first. If you belonged to the world, the world would love its own; but because you do not belong to the world, and I have chosen you out of the world, the world hates you" (John 15:18-19). Satan uses the weapons of hatred against Christ's own, and we ought to be consoled by the realization that we are being treated like our Master.

"Blessed are you," Jesus said, "when people hate you, and when they exclude and insult you and denounce your name as evil, on account of the Son of Man" (Luke 6:22). We ought, on the other hand, to feel uncomfortable if the world is ever happy with us, for Jesus said: "Woe to you when all speak well of you" (Luke 6:26).

In a very real sense, persecution should strengthen us in our willingness to evangelize. Jesus says that persecution leads to our "giving testimony" to him (Luke 21:13). Many converts to the Church, like Saint Paul in the first century and G.K Chesterton in the twentieth, were led to the Church because it was a target for persecution. People who are open to the truth will find the truth even when it is being attacked, and sometimes they will find it precisely because it is being attacked!

People open to the Holy Spirit may very well see that the Catholic Church is persecuted as Christ was persecuted, and recognize it as belonging to Christ. They will note that the Church is belittled as Christ was (John 7:41,52), and they will identify it as Christ's Church. They will observe that the Catholic Church is slandered as Christ was slandered (Mark 3:22), and they will identify it with Christ. They will detect that the world wants to destroy the Church as it once tried to destroy Christ on the cross, and they will come to know the Church as the Body of Christ.

When Christ was crucified by Evil , he rose from the dead. The Church, the Body of Christ, has risen from every cross of persecution throughout its history. We can be sure, as we proclaim Christ to a world which may at times be hostile, that the truth of Christ will prevail. Fortified by Christ's love, we will heed his admonition to "pray for those who persecute you" (Matthew 5:44). Strengthened by the certitude of Christ's promise, we will remain calm and assured in the spirit of Saint Peter: "Always be ready to give an explanation to anyone who asks you for a reason for your hope, but do it with gentleness and reverence, keeping your conscience clear, so that, when you are maligned, those who defame your good conduct in Christ may themselves be put to shame" (1 Peter 3:15-16).

Ecumenism and Evangelization

On the night before he died on the cross, Jesus prayed for his apostles. Then he said, "I pray not only for them, but also for those who will believe in me through their word, so that they may all be one, as you, Father, are in me and I in you, that they also may be in us, that the world may believe that you sent me" (John 17:20). Jesus gave the world a Church to teach in his name and to gather all people into one family, but he knew that some would reject his teaching and his Church.

From the very beginning, there have been disagreements among the followers of Christ. Often these disputes, by the grace of Christ's prayer, have been resolved. In the early Church, for example, there were serious disagreements about whether all believers had to accept Jewish laws and practices before they could become Christians. A "council" of apostles and Church leaders in Jerusalem (Acts 15) decided that this was not necessary, and the Church united in its willingness to accept converts from non-Jewish nations.

But at times, disagreements among Christ's followers have resulted in division and disunity. In New Testament times, for example, some people denied the Incarnation of Christ. They claimed to be "progressive," no doubt feeling that "intelligent people" could not believe that Jesus was both human and divine. Apparently, all efforts to bring such people back to the true Faith failed, for the author of the Second Letter of John had to warn his readers: "Anyone who is so 'progressive' as not to remain in the teaching of the Christ does not have God; whoever remains in the teaching has the Father and the Son. If anyone comes to you and does not bring this doctrine, do not receive him in your house or even greet him; for whoever greets him shares in his evil works" (2 John 9-11).

The worst divisions in Christian history have been those that occurred in 1054 when the Eastern churches separated from Rome and in the sixteenth century when Protestants broke away from unity with the Catholic Church. The causes for these divisions were many, and people on both sides were at fault. More recently, there have been numerous efforts to restore unity among churches, and the Second Vatican Council stated the desire of the Catholic Church to pray and work for unity.

The effort to achieve unity among the followers of Christ is called *ecumenism*. The official position of the Catholic Church toward this effort was explained in the *Decree on Ecumenism* issued by the Second Vatican Council. The Council states its belief that the Catholic Church is the true Church of Christ and the only Church where "the fullness of the means of salvation can be obtained." However, people in other Christian churches can be saved, for God uses these churches as a "means of salvation" for many. They are our brothers and sisters in Christ and have a real, though imperfect, union with the Catholic Church. There are significant differences in doctrine and discipline that present serious obstacles to full ecclesiastical communion, but all Catholics are encouraged to participate in the work of ecumenism. (SVC, *Ecumenism*, 3–4)

The work of ecumenism includes many things. We should avoid unfair attitudes and harmful language. Experts of different Christian churches can dialogue and so come to a better understanding of others. All can join in works of charity and social concern and come together in prayer. All can examine their own lives and strive to be faithful to Christ.

On the other hand, it would be a mistake to underestimate the differences among churches. Many sincere Christians have come to realize since the Council that true unity cannot be achieved by pretending that differences in belief are unimportant.

This is why the Catholic Church does not practice "inter-Communion." Many Protestants and some Catholics wonder why the Church does not invite all sincere people to receive Holy Communion. However, Holy Communion has always been a sign of *unity of belief* in the Catholic Church. In the early Church, people were not even allowed to attend the entire Mass until they had completed instructions and were baptized! For them, and for us, receiving Communion in the Catholic Church means this: "Through this Eucharist I am united with Jesus Christ and with all his members in the Catholic Church. I believe all the truths that the Church teaches and I am in full communion with the Catholic Church under the leadership of the Holy Father." Obviously, Holy Communion cannot have this meaning for those who are not Catholic. It is sad that we cannot all share Holy Communion together, but this is simply an expression of the fact that real divisions exist. We will solve nothing by trying to deprive Holy

Communion of the significance it has always had in the Catholic Church.

Doctrinal differences are important, and any efforts at ecumenism that ignore them are bound to fail. The road to full unity will be long and difficult, but it is a road that must be walked with courage, fidelity to the truth, and charity.

And with the help of the Holy Spirit, great strides have already been made. There have been dialogues at the highest levels. In large cities and small towns throughout Christianity, Catholics, Protestants, and others work together to help the poor. Ecumenical prayer services, especially at times like Easter and Thanksgiving, are common. Priests and ministers cooperate in ministerial alliances, praying together, meeting in friendship, and joining resources to serve the needy. Genuine love and respect govern relationships among individuals and churches.

In these ways, and in many others, Christ's prayer for unity is being answered. We, as Catholics, must be faithful to our beliefs, worship, and discipline, but we can continue to grow in the attitudes Christ surely wants us to have toward other Christians. In doing so, we are evangelizing, for there are millions of people in our world who belong to no church at all. If they see us treating others with understanding and respect, they will be drawn to us. "This is how all will know that you are my disciples, if you have love for one another" (John 13:35).

"Benedicamus Domino"

> Wherever the Catholic sun does shine,
> There's music, laughter, and good red wine.

In all the sacramental signs given by God and treasured by the Catholic Church, there is the music of God's voice telling the Good News of God's love and of our redemption by Jesus Christ. There is our laughter of the happiness at knowing Jesus, who guides us through a less than perfect world, and there is the laughter of the saints in heaven reminding us that our destiny is to enjoy forever the delight of seeing God face to face. There is the good red wine of the Eucharist and of all the sacraments and sacramental signs indicating that Jesus Christ is with us always until the end of time, and then forever.

"Let us bless the Lord!" To know our Catholic faith, to live it, and to teach others about it are blessings for which we praise God. We bless the Lord for the privilege of being Catholic and for the privilege of being called to share the Good News of Christ with all the world.

Questions for Discussion and Reflection

Have you ever considered it your responsibility to evangelize others? What are some practical ways in which you can share your faith with others? Have you ever been criticized because of your Catholic beliefs? What Catholic doctrines have you heard challenged? Do you feel better equipped to respond to attacks on the Catholic faith after reading this book? What ecumenical activities have you participated in? Do you pray and work for unity among Christians?

As you conclude this book, can you express in your own words the meaning of the "sacramental principle"? In what ways have your views and opinions of the Catholic Church been changed or developed by reading this book?

Activities

Spend some time in quiet prayer reflecting on the privilege of being Catholic. Then write down ten "privileges" of being Catholic that you consider most important. Say a prayer thanking God for the privilege of being Catholic and ask God to help you live your beliefs with courage and conviction.

Epilogue

The Catholic Church teaches that our lives matter. Catholicism proclaims that God takes away our sins and gives us grace, the spark of divine life, with the result that we can cooperate with God in performing good works and constructing of our years a life that counts. But we may not fully realize this. Sometimes we can be so overwhelmed by our own littleness and by our failures that we are tempted to discouragement.

We can be tempted also to discouragement when we view the Church today. We Catholics comprise a sixth of the world's population, but we are still a minority. There may be great people like Pope John Paul and Mother Teresa, but most of us don't seem to be all that important in the world's scheme of things. We seem to be so little and so weak as individuals, and we seem to be so little and so weak as a Church.

If that is how we feel about ourselves and about the Church, then we may need to view self and Church through the eyes of Christ. We can discern how Jesus sees us by examining how he saw the "little people" of his time. And the best way to learn the heart and mind of Christ may well be to study the story of the widow and her two coins as told in the Gospel of Mark:

> [Jesus] sat down opposite the treasury and observed how the crowd put money into the treasury. Many rich people put in large sums. A poor widow also came and put in two small coins worth a few cents. Calling his disciples to himself, he said to them, "Amen, I say to you, this poor widow put in more than all the other contributors to the treasury. For they have all contributed from their surplus wealth, but she, from her

poverty, has contributed all she had, her whole liveli-
hood."

Mark 12:41-44

Christ could see greatness where others saw only littleness and
poverty. I've often wondered why the widow put in her last two
coins and what her life was like. I've always felt that Jesus would
not have just talked about her, but that he would have gone to her
and told her what he told the apostles. I have written this short story
to describe what might have happened...

Rachel's Gift

Rachel trudged up the steps to the Court of the Women. Several
times she had to stop and catch her breath. Slowly, she made her
way toward the line of people waiting to make their donations to
the Temple. She joined it and slowly shuffled forward.

When she heard the clanging of heavy gold and silver coins
being dropped into the treasury, she almost gave up her place in
the line. "Heavenly Father," she prayed, "I'm just a foolish old
lady with almost nothing to give. But I promised you that if my
granddaughter gave birth to a healthy child, I would walk to
the Temple and make a donation to praise and thank you. I
didn't realize that all I had left in my box were these two copper
coins."

Rachel smiled at the thought of her first great-grandson. A
healthy boy! In spite of all the dangers the midwife had warned
about. In spite of her granddaughter's having to stay in bed for the
last three months of her pregnancy. *It is a miracle*, she thought.
God is so good.

"Lady," she heard a voice behind her, "Lady, the line is
moving." And her smile vanished in an instant as she remembered
where she was and the pitifulness of her predicament. An old
woman, barely able to walk, hobbling across this magnificent
Temple to donate...two copper coins. A tear trickled down her
cheek, but she plodded forward, hoping that no one would notice
her meager offering.

She glanced for a moment at the man just ahead of her. Fine
leather sandals, a beautiful robe, gold rings sparkling with jewels
on his fingers, an embroidered linen pouch heavy with coins in his

hand. He would make an offering worthy of this Temple with its majestic stone columns and ornamented porticoes.

Then she saw the rabbi, Jesus, who preached so beautifully of God's love. Everyone was talking about him. Many claimed to have seen him work miracles of healing. But now he was silent. Sitting not far from the treasury, he seemed to be looking over the crowds. "O dear heavenly Father," Rachel prayed, "please don't let Jesus see me." Then suddenly it was time for her gift. She fumbled in her purse for her coins. As quickly as she could, she dropped them into the treasury. The copper made a pitiful plinking sound that seemed to echo to the world the depths of her poverty and the littleness of her life.

Her eyes filled with tears. Shoulders sagging, she moved slowly through the crowd, wanting only to return home before she was swallowed up by her weariness and sorrow.

But someone was standing directly in her path. She looked for a moment into the face of Jesus, then hung her head in shame. "You saw me," she sobbed. "I'm so sorry. It was all I had. It was all I had."

Then she felt Jesus take her hands in his. He raised them up ever so slowly, until she was forced to look directly into his eyes. For a moment, Rachel was awed by the love and gentleness she saw in those eyes. "Rachel, Rachel," she heard the rabbi say. "Don't you understand what you have done? You have given more than all the others. You have given my heavenly Father everything you had. Everything! You kept nothing back. And now...now my Father will keep nothing back from you. Rachel, I used to be a carpenter, you know. And I still like to work with wood when I have the chance. This is something I whittled from a bit of branch, and I want you to have it." Jesus reached into a fold of his robe, took out a little object, and placed it in her hand. Then he was gone, lost in the Temple throngs.

Rachel waited until she was on a narrow back street, almost halfway home, before she looked at the gift. It was a lamb, no work of art, but carefully carved. *I'll keep it as long as I live,* she thought, *and I'll never forget his smile, or what he said.*

The walk home wasn't easy. For weeks, Rachel had felt a tightness around her heart. There were times when she could hardly breathe. But each time she sat down to rest, she looked at the little lamb and thought of David's psalm: "The Lord is my shepherd. There is nothing I shall want." Strengthened by the familiar words she had learned so long ago, she finally arrived at the little hut she called home.

That night Rachel had a dream. She was alone in a field, in unfamiliar surroundings. Then in the distance, she saw Jesus walking toward her. But this time his face was radiant as the sun. His robes were whiter than snow. He looked into her eyes as he had in the Temple. "I am the good shepherd," he said, and he took her by the hand.

They walked through a deep valley, where the only light seemed to come from Jesus. She held his hand tightly, and soon he was leading her into a beautiful city. She had never seen such glory! Then he paused before what seemed to be the grandest mansion of all. "There are many houses in my Father's kingdom, Rachel. And this one is yours."

The next morning Rachel's neighbor Anna was wondering why her old friend hadn't come over for hot tea and a little gossip. *I'd better check on her*, Anna thought. She knocked, hesitated, knocked again. No answer. Slowly, she opened the door.

The room was quite dark and very still. Not even the sound of breathing. As Anna's eyes began to adjust to the pattern of shadows cast from the open door, she saw Rachel lying on her bed. What first caught her attention was the look on Rachel's face. Then Anna noticed something else. She took Rachel's cold hand in her own and gently removed a small wooden carving....

"I've seen many a dead person," Anna would later relate to all she knew, "but never one with such a smile on her face."

As Christ Sees Us

When we are tempted to discouragement at the seeming littleness of our lives or at the weaknesses in our Catholic Church, we should remember Mark 12:41-44. If we do, we shall never despair. We shall never cease to work for the upbuilding of the Church made up of so many like ourselves. We shall never fail to realize that it is, indeed, a privilege to be Catholic.

In the beginning, "God looked at everything he had made, and he found it very good" (Genesis 1:31). Christ looks at everyone he has redeemed, and he who could treasure two copper coins must surely see the contribution of our lives joined in his Body, the Church, as very, very good.

Bibliography

Abbott, Walter, editor. *The Documents of Vatican II.* New York: Herder and Herder, 1966.

After Jesus—The Triumph of Christianity. Pleasantville, NY: Reader's Digest, 1992.

Book of Blessings. International Committee on English in the Liturgy, Washington, D.C.: United States Catholic Conference, 1988.

Catechism of the Catholic Church. United States Catholic Conference,1994.

Foster, Richard. *Celebration of Discipline: The Path to Spiritual Growth.* San Francisco: Harper San Francisco, 1988.

Foy, Felician A. and Avato, Rose M., eds. *Catholic Almanac.* Huntington, IN: Our Sunday Visitor, 1992.

Greeley, Andrew M. *American Catholics Since the Council.* Chicago: Thomas More Press, 1985.

_____. *The Catholic Myth: The Behavior and Beliefs of American Catholics.* New York: Collier Books, 1990. (Father Greeley's sociological studies, reported in this book, show conclusively that the sacramental principle [he calls it the sacramental imagination] is at the heart of Catholicism. His book helped me to understand the importance of the sacramental principle.)

Lukefahr, Oscar. *A Catholic Guide to the Bible.* Liguori, MO: Liguori Publications, 1992.

_____. *"We Believe..." A Survey of the Catholic Faith.* Liguori, MO: Liguori Publications, 1990.

Neuhaus, Richard I. *The Catholic Moment.* San Francisco: Harper San Francisco, 1987.

New American Bible. Brookville, NY: Catholic Book Publisher, 1970, 1989, 1991.

New Catholic Encyclopedia. New York: McGraw-Hill Book Company, 1967.

Sisters of St. Joseph of Philadelphia. *Encyclopedic Dictionary of Religion.* Washington, D.C.: Corpus Publications, 1979.

Tracy, David. *The Analogical Imagination.* New York: Crossroad, 1985.

Ward, J. Neville. *Five for Sorrow, Ten for Joy: A Consideration of the Rosary.* Revised Edition. Cambridge, MA, Cowley Publications, 1985.

Index